Getting the Teachers We Need

Getting the Teachers We Need

*International Perspectives
on Teacher Education*

Edited by Sharon Feiman-Nemser
and Miriam Ben-Peretz

Editorial Committee:
Shlomo Back, Ariela Gordon,
and Sarah Shimoni

The
MOFET Institute
Research, Curriculum and Program Development for
Teacher Educators

ROWMAN & LITTLEFIELD
Lanham • Boulder • New York • London

Published by Rowman & Littlefield
A wholly owned subsidiary of The Rowman & Littlefield Publishing Group, Inc.
4501 Forbes Boulevard, Suite 200, Lanham, Maryland 20706
www.rowman.com

Unit A, Whitacre Mews, 26-34 Stannary Street, London SE11 4AB

British Library Cataloguing in Publication Information Available

Library of Congress Cataloging-in-Publication Data

978-1-4758-2962-4 (cloth : alk. paper)
978-1-4758-2963-1 (pbk. : alk. paper)
978-1-4758-2964-8 (electronic)

♾ ™ The paper used in this publication meets the minimum requirements of American National Standard for Information Sciences Permanence of Paper for Printed Library Materials, ANSI/NISO Z39.48-1992.

Printed in the United States of America

Contents

Foreword

As the focus on education across the globe becomes increasingly sharp, it is little wonder that teacher education has attracted more and more attention, not just for what it does in preparing teachers, but also for what it might do differently.

Education is commonly seen as a way to create opportunities for people to take more control of their own destiny and to improve their standard of living. Curiously though, in the Western World in particular, teachers appear to be undervalued and the conception of teacher education is too often reduced to a simple training model designed to produce "classroom ready teachers" (TEMAG, 2014). The difficulty with this situation is that the product sought from teacher education is largely shaped by views of teaching that revolve around the delivery of information or transmissive approaches to teaching (Barnes, 1976).

Despite Freire's (1972) critique of the "banking model" of teaching and learning, when "push comes to shove," teaching is still largely seen as the delivery of information ameliorated through well-honed performance. Sadly, such a view ignores the knowledge, skills, and abilities central to quality in teaching and masks what expert teachers know and are able to do (Loughran, 2010). The same applies to teacher educators, the teachers of teachers, who by all that they do are in some way or another held responsible for the way teachers teach throughout their careers.

So what does teacher education do and how might it be done differently? This book, which has been so thoughtfully organized and constructed by the editors, offers ways of seeing into teacher education anew. The volume responds to such things as the economic limitations associated with "fast track" routes to teacher certification while also considering challenges such as the introduction of technology, teaching core instructional practices, as well as the place and nature of teacher education in preparing teachers for an ever-changing world.

The organization of schooling is based on an industrial model of development and production. This is increasingly challenged by the need for creative, adaptive, and entrepreneurial learners capable of challenging and re-creating expectations around curriculum, teaching, and learning in response to the fast paced digital age. Learning should not be constrained by classroom walls; it needs to be able to break free. That requires teachers who are comfortable with the uncertainty of working in what Schön (1983) so aptly described as the swampy lowlands of practice, a space that cannot easily be mapped nor precisely navigated.

As many scholars have noted over the years, teaching may look easy (Labaree, 2000), but looks can be deceiving. As Lortie's (1975) "apprenticeship of observation" well illustrates, teacher education can be similarly mis-interpreted to the detriment of genuinely seeing and understanding the complexity what the teaching of teaching entails (Cochran-Smith, 2005; Darling-Hammond, 2013; Davey, 2013; Korthagen, Loughran, & Lunenberg, 2005; Swennen & van der Klink, 2009).

In response to the myriad expectations, hopes, and demands on teaching and teacher education, the chapters in this book make clear that it is not so much that prospective teachers or the process of teacher education as a process require radical overhaul. Rather it is more a matter of understanding what might reasonably be expected in preparing teachers who can nurture learning in their students in ways that appropriately respond to the context, content, hopes, and possibilities associated with developing able, responsible, and active learners.

For example, the notion of "fast tracking" academically able candidates into teacher education may be initiated by good intentions, but if it is limited by understandings of teaching as the "delivery of information," then the sophisticated nature of teaching is eschewed and the resultant practice does little to challenge the status quo of schooling.

In a similar way, the location of teacher education should not be seen as the governing factor for the way that teacher education is organized and structured.

The ability of well-informed and highly capable teacher educators to open up for scrutiny the problematic nature of teaching for students of teaching is not confined to universities or practice settings as mutually exclusive sites. Teacher education through residency or third space possibilities is about making the problematic recognizable, clear, and manageable for students of teaching. In so doing, the daily routines of teaching can be "unpacked" and examined in ways that challenge the notion of teaching as a script and offer new ways of helping beginning teachers feel comfortable with the uncertainty inherent in managing pedagogy in meaningful ways (Loughran, 2013).

There is clearly a need for teachers to refine their core practices and expertly support their students' learning, though that is dramatically different from rigidly adhering to generalized, pre-defined "teacher-proof" training protocols. Expert teachers develop skills, knowledge, and abilities that allow them to see beyond the "doing of teaching" into the purposes of practice. They become adept at recognizing, responding, adapting, and innovating as they see beyond the "what and how" of practice and into the why which rightly directs and informs that practice. If teaching is to be understood as complex and sophisticated work, then teacher education must be seen as an important beginning point, offering a vision for the professional learning and development of a teacher's professional knowledge and practice.

As the chapters in this book illustrate, teacher education faces challenges that are immediate and demanding. Adapting teacher education to the changing needs of educational systems is an imperative, an imperative that lies at the heart of what teaching and learning is all about. This book offers engaging, thoughtful, and sometimes provocative ways of engaging in the debate around what is and can be in teacher education, while not ignoring the how and why.

As some of her recent work attests, Ben-Peretz (2011) continues to examine teaching and teacher education in ways that invite us all to take seriously what it means to build and support the profession of teaching. Feiman-Nemser (2014) does the same in her recent book which offers close-up studies of three mission-driven, context-specific teacher education programs and their effects on teachers. In collaborating on this book, the editors and authors continue that challenge, asking us all to think again about what we do, how, and why, as we seek to engender quality in teaching and teacher education in these ever-changing times.

—*John Loughran, dean of education, Monash University, Australia*

REFERENCES

Barnes, D. (1976). *From communication to curriculum*. Harmondsworth: Penguin.

Ben-Peretz, M., Kleeman, S., Reichenberg, R., & Shimoni, S. (Eds.). (2013). *Teacher educators as members of an evolving profession*. New York: Rowman & Littlefield Education.

Cochran-Smith, M. (2005). Teacher educators as researchers: Multiple perspectives. *Teaching and Teacher Education, 21*, 219–225.

Darling-Hammond, L. (2013). Building a profession of teaching: Teacher educators as change agents. In M. Ben-Peretz, S. Kleeman, R. Reichenberg, & S. Shimoni (Eds.), *Teacher educators as members of an evolving profession* (pp. 87–102). New York: Rowman & Littlefield Education.

Davey, R. L. (2013). *The professional identity of teacher educators: Career on the cusp?* London: Routledge.

Feiman-Nemser, S., Tamir, E., & Hammerness, K. (2014). *Inspiring teaching: Preparing teachers to succeed in mission driven schools*. Cambridge, MA: Harvard Education Press.

Freire, P. (1972). *Pedagogy of the oppressed*. New York: Herder & Herder.

Korthagen, F. A. J., Loughran, J. J., & Lunenberg, M. (2005). Teaching teachers: Studies into the expertise of teacher educators. *Teaching and Teacher Education, 21*(2), 107–115.

Labaree, D. F. (2000). On the nature of teaching and teacher education: Difficult practices that look easy. *Journal of Teacher Education, 51*, 228–233.

Loughran, J. J. (2010). *What expert teachers do: Teachers' professional knowledge of classroom practice*. London: Allen & Unwin.

Loughran, J. J. (2013). Pedagogy: Making sense of the complex relationship between teaching and learning. *Curriculum Inquiry, 43*(1), 118–141.

Schön, D. A. (1983). *The reflective practitioner: How professionals think in action*. New York: Basic Books.

TEMAG. (2014). *Action now: Classroom ready teachers*. Canberra: Department of Education.

Acknowledgments

We are grateful to the people whose assistance was vital for this book. Special thanks to Tom Koerner, vice president and editorial director of Rowman & Littlefield, and to Michal Golan, head of the MOFET Institute, for their encouragement, advice, and help. Thanks also to Tali Aderet-German for her invaluable assistance.

We also express our sincere appreciation to John Loughran for writing the foreword to this book. Thanks also to Yehudit Shteiman, head of Writing Channel and head of MOFET's Publication House, Hanni Shushtari, coordinator of MOFET's Publication House, and Carlie Wall, assistant editor, Rowman & Littlefield, Education Division, for their help in preparing this book. Finally, our appreciation to all the authors for their cooperation in this endeavor.

Alternative Approaches to Teacher Education

What Differences Make a Difference?

Sharon Feiman-Nemser

Research confirms what personal experience reveals—that teachers make an important difference in the learning and life chances of children and youth. While all children deserve to be taught by effective teachers, ensuring an adequate supply of such teachers especially for hard-to-staff schools and high-demand subjects is a pressing social challenge in many national contexts. The lack of consensus about the best way to recruit, prepare, develop, and retain good teachers exacerbates the problem.

The proliferation of teacher education programs and pathways to teaching reflects this. In the last twenty-five years, the growth of alternate routes to teaching has radically altered the landscape of teacher education. No longer must aspiring teachers attend a college or university program to earn a teaching certificate. While most teachers are still prepared in post-secondary institutions, people interested in teaching have many more choices for how to enter the field.

Some view the explosion of different routes to teaching as a positive sign of choice in a free market. Others view it as an expression of innovation and responsiveness to changing economic and social conditions. Still others see the growth of alternative programs as a critique of the traditional providers of teacher education, namely colleges and universities, and the professional organizations which accredit their programs.

Criticism of teacher education has a long history, but so do innovation and experimentation. Alternatives in teacher education have always existed because teacher educators, policy makers, teachers, school leaders, and researchers disagree about what constitutes the best education for teachers. Today, however, the criticism seems sharper and the debates more polarizing in the face of changing demographics, growing inequality, globalization and neo-liberal policies. These developments have led to an unprecedented focus on teacher quality and accountability as educators and policy makers strive to expand access, reduce the achievement gap and raise standards for all.

How do we get the teachers we need? Like programs in the past, contemporary teacher education programs represent different responses to this basic question. For some the answer lies in recruiting academically talented and/or socially conscious candidates. For others the answer lies in providing serious professional preparation informed by a growing understanding of teaching and learning. Still others advocate a combination of targeted recruitment, robust preparation and ongoing development.

One frequently hears comparisons of traditional and alternate route teacher education. In recent years, however, researchers have challenged this distinction on the grounds that differences within the broad categories are as great as differences between them (Grossman & Loeb, 2008; National Research Council, 2011). Two questions come to mind: Is there such a thing as a traditional teacher education program, and How can we meaningfully distinguish different approaches to teacher education?

When people refer to a "traditional" pre-service program, they generally have in mind a four-year, undergraduate program. Historian of education Lawrence Cremin (1978) attributes the model to James Earl Russell, dean of Teachers College at Columbia University between 1884 and 1927, who argued that a proper curriculum for teachers should include general culture, special scholarship, professional knowledge, and technical skills. The basic outline of Russell's curriculum is reflected in the familiar components of a typical undergraduate sequence—general education including academic majors and minors, professional studies consisting of courses in foundations and pedagogy, and student teaching. Unfortunately the letter more than the spirit of Russell's conception has endured.

Reforms in teacher education tend to focus on structures, pitting one institutional form against another. In the past this meant normal schools versus teachers colleges and undergraduate versus graduate programs. In recent years it means traditional versus alternate route programs. The tendency to confuse structure and substance and to link program quality with particular institutional arrangements is misleading. Indeed the popularity of a given form of teacher preparation may have more to do with prevailing social and economic trends than the strengths or weaknesses of the form itself.

This book explores alternatives in teacher education by featuring programs that represent popular contemporary models and developments. One contribution is to show some of the variation within as well as across broad program types. Another is to highlight core questions that all teacher education programs confront.

ALTERNATE ROUTES TO TEACHING

Programs in this category are variously called "alternate route," "fast-track," "employment-based" and "alternative certification" programs. The first label signals a departure from "traditional" university or college-based teacher education. The second highlights the brief preparation candidates receive before they become teachers of record. The third signals the fact that candidates are employed by a school system where they learn to teach on the job. The fourth highlights the fact that these pathways lead to regular as opposed to emergency certification.

Alternate route programs have sparked heated debates inside and outside the teacher education community. Often these debates pit supporters of serious professional preparation against advocates of targeted, selective recruitment. The former believe that teaching is a complex professional practice which must be learned and can be taught. Furthermore it is unethical to place people in classrooms, especially classrooms serving poor minority students, who have not been prepared for responsible beginning teaching. The latter believe that most of what teachers need to know can be learned on the job. If we recruit academically able, second career or minority candidates with a background in their teaching subject(s), they can figure out how to teach while teaching.

Today, alternative paths to teacher certification come in many different shapes and sizes. Teach For America (TFA), the most familiar, offers selective recruitment, brief preparation, and on-the-job support. The TFA model has expanded across the United States and inspired Teach For All, a global network in thirty-six countries. The chapters about alternate route programs examine their political and ideological underpinnings, trace their impact on university and school-based teacher educators, and illustrate how the original template has been adapted in different national contexts.

New Jersey's Alternate Route

Eran Tamir analyzes the political transformations and complex motivations which led to the first "fast-track" program in the United States. During the 1980s, rising concerns about the United States losing its economic standing in the world led to harsh criticisms of schools and teachers for failing to meet high academic standards. New Jersey's newly elected Republican governor, Tom Kean, promoted a neo-liberal agenda and mission to improve the quality of teachers. A coalition led by the governor and the Commissioner of

Education pushed through an alternate route policy rooted in market values of choice and competition.

Tamir argues that New Jersey's alternate route program, which he characterizes as "brief preparation and thin support," was never fully justified on educational grounds. At the same time, the New Jersey program and those which followed have stimulated extensive discussion and debate about teacher quality; prompted research on teacher recruitment, preparation, retention and assessment; and led to significant developments and improvements in teacher preparation.

SchoolDirect, England

Compared to Tamir's even-handed assessment, Murray, Czerniawski, and Kidd see mostly negative consequences flowing from market-driven teacher education policies in England. They focus on the controversial School Direct, a government-sponsored, employment-based initial teacher-training initiative launched in 2010. In this program, schools recruit college or university graduates who want to become teachers, provide their field experience, and arrange any other training the school deems necessary.

The swift spread of School Direct took teacher educators in higher education by surprise, undermining their expertise and transforming them into managers of school partnerships and marketers of training contracts. Yet Murray et al. also see the potential for new practices to emerge from these reconfigured spaces of teacher education as long as school, and university-based teacher educators focus on improving the quality of student teacher learning rather than competing with other providers.

Hotam Naomi, Israel

The Hotam Naomi program aims to strengthen the teaching profession in Israel by recruiting and preparing "activist teacher leaders" who will teach for at least two years in the weakest schools in the geographic and social periphery. Part of the international Teach For All network, this highly competitive program recruits a heterogeneous group of candidates including Jews, Christians, and Arabs; men and women; Israeli born and immigrants from different regions of the country and different fields of academic study.

The program is a partnership between the Hotam organization and two academic institutions. Initially the institutional partners had different views about what the program should be like. Out of their disagreements and deliberations, a new curriculum emerged, attuned to the trajectories of new teacher learning and the rhythms of the school year, and focused on "relevant issues, significant theory, and a common vision" (chapter 3).

TeachFirst, New Zealand

A similar vision animates TeachFirst NZ, an employment-based secondary teacher education program created in 2011 to meet the needs of underserved students in New Zealand, most notably Maori and Pasifika. The program is a partnership between a fledgling charitable trust and the University of Auckland, a faculty with long experience in initial teacher education. According to the Dean of the College of Education, the program aims to make teaching in low decile schools a positive choice.

Like other programs of its kind, TeachFirst NZ involves rigorous selection, intensive summer preparation before students take on not quite full-time teaching, provision of just-in-time teaching and learning strategies, and in-school mentoring. Other features of the program, such as the integration of theory and practice, an emphasis on culturally responsive pedagogy, a view of teaching as inquiry, and the development of a community of practice, reflect ideas about effective teacher education in general (Darling-Hammond & Bransford, 2005).

The Israeli Project for Excellent Students

Over the last twenty years, Israel has invested considerable funds in efforts to attract academically talented people to teaching. One experiment, the Israeli Project for Excellent Students (IESP), offers full scholarships to academically talented high school graduates to attend a college of education where they complete their academic requirements and earn a teaching credential. Participants take the same program as other students, but they can complete it in three rather than four years. They also participate in a variety of enrichment opportunities.

According to Tzipora Libman, teachers who participated in the IESP project remain in teaching at exactly the same rate as teachers in a control group (60% of teachers from both groups were still teaching after six years). This finding challenges a widespread belief that academically able teachers tend to leave teaching more frequently than other teachers.

Whether IESP counts as an alternate route to teaching is an open question. Like other alternate route programs, it relies on a rigorous and selective recruitment process in the belief that attracting academically talented people will improve the quality and perhaps the stature of teaching. It also offers an accelerated path to teaching. Still, the core program does not differ from the program offered to "regular" education students.

URBAN TEACHER RESIDENCY PROGRAMS

Urban teacher residencies (UTRs) have become increasingly popular in the last twenty years. The model, which has attracted substantial public and philanthropic funding in the United States, is gaining traction abroad. Some urban teacher residency programs exist outside universities; others depend on partnerships between universities and school districts. Most involve selective recruitment, a focus on high-needs schools, a full-year "residency" in the classroom of an experienced teacher who is also a trained mentor, integration of masters level coursework with classroom practice, and continuing support for graduates once they become teachers of record.

Montclair/Newark Urban Teacher Residency

Established with a grant from the U.S. Department of Education, the Newark/Montclair Urban Teacher Residency (NMUTR) prepares secondary math and science teachers. Program leaders sought to enact a "radical vision of teacher education" by situating the program in a "third space" between the university and the schools. The twelve-month program combines teacher preparation, teacher leadership, and school change.

Residents come from diverse ethnic, linguistic, and socio-economic backgrounds. They must have an undergraduate degree in mathematics or science. They are expected to teach in the Newark Public Schools for at least three years.

Taylor and Klein describe program features which enable residents to develop authentic relationships with urban youth, learn about the strengths and needs of the community, and design math and science curricula with social justice themes. They also discuss how mentor teachers learn to play a central role in residents' learning.

The "third space" metaphor highlights the work of negotiating new roles and relationships between universities and schools. Such work avoids traditional hierarchies and challenges traditional assumptions about the locus of different kinds of knowledge. Efforts to redefine university-school relationships in teacher education is a recurring theme in this book.

PRACTICE-CENTERED TEACHER EDUCATION

If urban teacher residency programs situate new teacher learning *in* practice, practice-based teacher education focuses teacher education *on* a set of core teaching practices essential for responsible beginning teaching. Practice-centered programs provide opportunities for pre-service candidates to learn these practices in conjunction with knowledge, skills, and commitments needed to enact them. The movement responds to current efforts to hold teacher educators accountable for the competence of their graduates (Ball & Forzani, 2009).

Francesca Forzani discusses how Teachingworks, located at the University of Michigan, identified nineteen "high-leverage" teaching practices based in a vision of good teaching and learning. These core practices became the foundation for redesigning the undergraduate elementary pre-service program around three strands: (1) teaching practice, (2) content knowledge for teaching, and (3) professional ethical obligations. In all three strands, students' learning takes place in on-campus courses and related field experiences, with the content for strands two and three derived from the core practices that make up strand one.

Karen Hammerness and Bill Kennedy offer rich descriptions of practice-centered teacher education as enacted in their preservice programs—the Bard College Master of Arts in Teaching (MAT) program and the University of Chicago's Urban Teacher Education Program (Chicago UTEP). Each program prepares teachers for a specific, large urban school district. Their descriptions challenge the critique that practice-centered teacher education is technical because it disconnects practice from broader purposes, understandings, and commitments (Zeichner, 2012).

Hammerness describes how pre-service candidates learn to create democratic classrooms rooted in a vision of good teaching and theories of learning. Kennedy describes how pre-service candidates learn to engage in productive dialogue with stakeholders of urban schools, informed by ideas about race, equity, culturally relevant pedagogy, and funds of knowledge. Their extended examples illustrate the teaching of core practices in relation to foundational knowledge and a vision of good teaching.

SPECIAL CHALLENGES: TECHNOLOGY AND INCLUSION

As technology transforms our world, our educational system, and our individual lives, the place of technology in teacher education is receiving increasing attention. Jae-Eun Joo and Bob Moon argue that digital technologies can help reconfigure the relationship between universities and schools. Margo Pensavalle, Melora Sundt, and Karen Gallagher describe the first online Master of Arts in Teaching (MAT) program at the University of Southern California (USC). While technology enables USC to extend its reach, it has not (yet) produced the reconfigured relationships between universities and schools that Joo and Moon predict.

Joo and Moon describe digital resources used by teacher educators around the world, including Open Educational Resources, MOOCs, flipped classrooms, marketspaces, and wearable technologies. They suggest that these technologies offer new ways to connect the university and the schools which are traditionally separated by geography, culture, and logistics. They claim that blending face-to-face communication with more networked modes of working can foster less hierarchical relationships between these two institutions.

Redefined relationships between university and schools is not a prominent theme in the story of how the University of Southern California created an online MAT program in partnership with a for-profit technology company. Penavalle, Sundt, and Gallagher describe the program's guiding assumptions, "developmental" structure, and modes of delivery, which involve synchronous classes, practice teaching placements in schools close to where students live, and the use of social media to form professional communities. They also identify some of the challenges, including difficulties implementing a strong student-teaching component and problems establishing clear boundaries and expectations with their entrepreneurial partner.

Rony Lidor identifies three contemporary challenges facing teacher educators—technology, multiculturalism, and inclusion. Focusing on the third, he describes how the Zinman College of Physical Education and Sport Sciences in Israel tackled the challenge of integrating physically disabled students into its teacher preparation program. Although the program requires creative adjustments on many levels, it has touched both the disabled teacher candidates as well as the student volunteers who assist them.

WHAT DIFFERENCES MAKE A DIFFERENCE?

Each of these programs represents a response to the question, "How can we get the teachers we need?" In developing their response, programs had to decide which candidates to recruit, what content to teach, how to structure and support teacher learning, and when and where the learning would take place. Reviewing how different programs answer these questions reveals the hybrid nature of many.

Most of the programs sought to change the demographics of the teaching force. Usually this meant recruiting academically able candidates, but it also meant recruiting candidates with relevant life or work experience, particular academic majors, diverse racial and ethnic backgrounds, and/or a strong commitment to social justice. These recruitment policies reflect implicit or explicit beliefs about the kinds of people likely to make good teachers in particular contexts.

All teacher education programs must decide what teachers need to learn and what programs can teach within the available time. One research-based framework suggests that prospective teachers need to develop (a) a vision of good teaching to inspire and guide their learning and practice; (b) knowledge of the subject(s) they will teach; (c) an understanding of learners and learning, including students' cultures and communities; (d) a basic repertoire for planning, instruction, assessment and management; and (e) the skills and commitment to continue developing their practice (Feiman-Nemser, 2001).

Few chapters explicitly discuss subject matter knowledge for teaching. This omission does not necessarily mean a lack of attention to teachers' subject matter knowledge, but it raises the question of how different programs address this fundamental requirement. Mainly programs rely on teachers' academic background as reflected in their college major(s). We know, however, that this is an unreliable proxy.

One area that does receive explicit attention is learning about learners, their cultures and communities. Many of the programs described here prepare teachers for schools with high percentages of poor, minority students. This may explain the shared commitment to help teachers reject deficit views of poor students in favor of seeing all students as capable learners from families and communities with unique strengths and resources. While some alternate routes rely on teaching experience to catalyze learning about students and their cultural backgrounds, other programs provide a sequence of carefully structured investigations and community-based learning opportunities paired with appropriate readings and personal reflections.

How do the various programs define a beginning repertoire for teachers and help novices learn to enact such a repertoire? Practice-centered programs address the question directly by organizing teacher learning around a set of "high-leverage practices" deemed essential for responsible beginning teaching. Advocates claim that collective agreement about core practices of teaching would strengthen the field of teacher education.

Too often teacher educators teach *about* new kinds of teaching without helping teacher candidates learn how to enact such teaching. The traditional approach to this "problem of enactment" (Kennedy, 1999) is student teaching, a time to apply what was supposedly learned at the university. The "pitfalls of experience" in student teaching are all too familiar (Feiman-Nemser & Buchmann, 1985). They also apply to learning on-the-job without a guiding vision of good teaching and opportunities for modeling, coaching, and feedback (Ronfeldt, 2010).

"Clinical" and "practice-centered" teacher education take different approaches to the problem of enactment. Associated with urban teacher residencies, clinical teacher education emphasizes intensive and extensive guided practice integrated with coursework. In practice-centered teacher education, teacher educators design learning opportunities in the context of university courses where teacher candidates analyze and rehearse core practices with coaching and feedback before trying to enact them under real classroom conditions.

A related question is whether to prepare teachers for schools as they are or schools as they ought to be. Too often beginning teachers feel caught between the vision of reform-minded teaching advocated by their teacher education program and the kind of teaching encountered in the schools where they teach and learn to teach. Several programs take on the dual challenge of helping novices learn to work in schools as they are while also becoming teacher leaders and agents of change.

Partnerships emerge as another cross-program theme. Many of the programs are products of partnerships between universities and schools or universities and for-profit or not-for-profit organizations. Some use the metaphor of a "third space" to signal the work of reconceptualizing roles and relationships between these institutions.

One obvious difference among the various programs relates to the scope and location of the preparation offered. New teachers inevitably learn on the job; however, the nature and intensity of that learning varies. A number of programs offer one to three years of on-the-job support and guidance, thereby linking or blurring the boundaries between initial preparation and new teacher induction. This is true for accelerated programs as well as for multi-year, clinically rich programs, another reminder that distinctions between traditional and alternate routes do not always hold.

So what differences make a difference? Instead of relying on comparisons of broad program types, researchers now call for studies which identify program features that lead to effective teaching and learning (Grossman & Loeb, 2008). In one large-scale study, researchers found the following features were associated with graduates' impact on student achievement: (a) courses in teachers' content area; (b) careful oversight of student teaching; (c) a focus on helping candidates learn specific teaching practices; (d) opportunities to learn about local district curricula; and (e) student teaching aligned with later teaching assignments (Boyd, Grossman, Lankford, Loeb, & Wykoff, 2008).

Teachers generally regard field experience as the most useful part of their preparation. Consequently, researchers have been studying how particular aspects of student teaching—the placement site, the selection and training of mentors, the quality of modeling and guidance, the relationship of the site to the program's vision of good teaching and the kind of school where graduates intend to teach—influence teacher effectiveness (Rondfelt, 2010).

As policy makers and researchers shift their focus from inputs (e.g., qualifications of candidates and faculty) to outcomes (e.g., teaching performance, student achievement, teacher retention), we need to remember that such outcomes result from the interaction of teacher, program, and school setting. To understand the quality of teacher education and its effects, we need to probe how different combinations of this central dynamic affect teacher learning, practice, and retention (Feiman-Nemser, Tamir, and Hammerness, 2014).

Research on the relationship between features of teacher education and student learning is in its infancy, and most aspects of this relationship are not well understood. As we build this knowledge base, teacher educators can also learn from the thinking and practice of thoughtful teacher educators. Hopefully this introduction has provoked readers' interest in learning more about the alternative programs featured here and has provided some critical lens for thinking about what differences make a difference.

REFERENCES

Ball, D., & Forzani, R. (2009). The work of teaching and the challenge for teacher education. *Journal of Teacher Education, 60*(5), 497–511.

Boyd, D., Grossman, P., Curtis, R., Hernandez, M., Wurtzel, J., & Snyder, J. (2008). *Creating and sustaining urban teacher residencies.* Chapel Hill, NC: The Aspen Institute and Center for Teaching Quality.

Cremin, L. (1978). *The education of the educating professions.* Paper presented at the American Association of Colleges for Teacher Education.

Darling-Hammond, L., & Bransford, J. (2005). *Preparing teachers for a changing World.* San Francisco, CA: Jossey-Bass.

Feiman-Nemser, S. (2001). From preparation to practice: Designing a continuum to strengthen and sustain teaching. *Teachers College Record, 103*(6), 1013–1055.

Feiman-Nemser, S., & Buchman, M. (1985). Pitfalls of experience in teacher preparation. *Teachers College Record, 87*(1), 53–65.

Feiman-Nemser, S., Tamir, E., & Hammerness, K. (2014). *Inspiring teaching: Preparing teachers to succeed in mission-driven schools.* Cambridge, MA: Harvard Education Press.

Grossman, P., & Loeb, S. (Eds.). (2008). *Alternative routes to teaching: Mapping the new landscape of teacher education.* Cambridge, MA: Harvard Education Press.

Kennedy, M. (1999). The role of preservice teacher education. In L. Darling-Hammond and G. Sykes (Eds.), *Teaching as the Learning Profession: Handbook of Teaching and Policy.* San Francisco: Jossey-Bass.

National Research Council. (2011). *Preparing teachers.* Washington, DC: National Academies Press.

Ronfeldt, M. (2010). Where should student teachers learn to teach? Effects of field placement school characteristics on teacher retention and effectiveness. *Educational Evaluation and Policy Analysis, 34*(1), 3–26.

Zeichner, K. (2012). The turn once again toward practice-based teacher education. *Journal of Teacher Education, 63*(5), 376–382.

Chapter One

The First Alternate Route to Teacher Certification in the United States

Realities and Misconceptions

Eran Tamir

Teaching has long been considered a fragile profession with teachers' authority scrutinized and governed by multiple stakeholders. This includes local school boards, administrators, state officials (Tamir, 2008), and more recently, the federal Department of Education and various national organizations, like professional networks, think tanks and advocacy groups. Some sociologists argue that because teachers lack the public legitimacy necessary to govern themselves (Abbott, 1988), teaching is more accurately understood as a semi-profession or at least, a public profession constrained by its enormous size, social function, and subordination to the nation-state.

One key aspect of authority that professional groups aspire to hold is the power to regulate the supply of professionals by certifying newcomers and controlling the licensure process. Teachers have spent considerable resources trying to control and shape the licensure process according to their professional interests. For example, at the turn of the twentieth century, teachers collaborated successfully with state politicians and officials to abolish local control and revamp the teacher licensure process.

Instead of teachers being recruited and retained by local school boards based on subjective criteria like personal values and family reputation, teachers supported the use of supposedly clear, universal criteria based on objective meritocratic principles like college recommendations for program completers and candidates' performance on standardized tests (Sedlak, 2008).[1]

Teachers and state officials needed the professional expertise and scientific authority of educational researchers in colleges of education to legitimate this new teacher-licensing model (Tamir, 2008). The loosely coupled alliance of interests among state officials, teachers and teacher unions, and educational researchers and scholars lasted through the late 1970s (Tamir, 2008).

Around that time, the alliance started to crack, leading once again to a struggle over what teachers need to know and who should define and take responsibility for teacher preparation and certification. This is the background to our story about the creation of the first alternate route to teacher certification in the United States. It reflects an ongoing battle over the teaching profession's right to define its boundaries and decide what knowledge professional teachers need and where and how they should acquire it.

This chapter situates the establishment of the first alternate route to certification in the United States in larger political transformations during the early 1980s which shaped debates over public education and teaching. It focuses on New Jersey's alternate route to teaching, discussing the realities and misconceptions that led to the alternate route policy. It also draws lessons and implications for the teaching profession in general and teacher preparation and certification in particular.

THE CHANGING POLITICAL AND IDEOLOGICAL LANDSCAPE OF EDUCATIONAL POLICY

One cannot understand the establishment of the first fast-track alternate route to teaching in the United States without acknowledging the larger political context at the time. As President Lyndon Johnson's War on Poverty faded away and decades of continuous economic prosperity halted, the political order was shaken. During the 1970s, Republican criticism about the inefficient and wasteful public sector became increasingly popular. Inspired by neo-liberal thinkers like Milton Friedman and by neo-conservative demands that America re-assert its role as a superpower, Republican Ronald Reagan won a landslide victory over the incumbent Democratic president Jimmy Carter.

Although public education was not a top priority for Republicans, it fit well with neo-liberal demands for open competition and choice, and with neo-conservative concerns about the failure of the nation's schools to produce excellent scientists and engineers to preserve the economic and military lead against foreign powers. In 1983, the Reagan administration charged the National Commission on Excellence in Education to determine a new course of action for public schools.

The Commission's landmark report, *A Nation at Risk* (National Commission on Excellence in Education, 1983), was the most prominent and politicized of the high profile reports which appeared during the decade. The Commission sharply criticized American public schools, arguing that student achievement had been rapidly deteriorating, partly because under-qualified teachers were being recruited and poorly prepared for their job.

The Reagan administration helped to reshape discourse on public education by promoting and spreading new ideas like "choice in education" through school vouchers and charter schools.[2] As part of the neo-liberal economic agenda, it fought hard to break down organized labor (Tamir, 2008). Teacher unions were painted as self-serving interest groups concerned with maintaining their benefits and power, even if doing that resulted in inefficiencies, spread mediocrity, and failed to serve parents, students, and the larger economy.

The Political Context of New Jersey

While larger political and ideological transformations at the federal level are important, decisions about education mainly happen at the state level. Thus, in order to understand why and how the alternate route evolved in New Jersey, we need to consider several important milestones in the history and politics of education in that state.[3]

For starters, politics and more specifically the ability to exert power are directly related to the availability of state funding. For most of its history, New Jersey collected few taxes, which meant it was unable to fund educational reform. Instead, education remained the prerogative of local governments, a system that preserved social and economic inequality. In the 1970s, New Jersey changed its tax code. The considerable growth in its budget which made state intervention in public education possible (Salmore & Salmore, 1993).

When Republican Thomas Kean was elected governor in 1892, he made education a key priority. The prosperity of the 1980s and changes in the tax code funneled unprecedented amounts to the state's coffers, allowing Governor Kean to explore new, untested ideas in education policy. The alternate route program fit with neo-liberal ideas at the time. It promoted a vision of free and open markets and the elimination of monopolistic power and barriers maintained by self-serving professional groups (Klagholz, 2000).

The types of players involved and their relationships also played a key role in advancing this policy. The alternate route policy succeeded because teacher educators, who stood the most to lose, were the weakest group in the field of education (e.g., Tamir, 2008). The governor offered a sweet deal to the powerful state teachers' union by proposing a big salary hike for beginning teachers in exchange for their support of the alternate route. In addition, internal frictions between the state teachers' union and the union representing teacher educators worked against building a cohesive front against the state.

THE ALTERNATE ROUTE TO TEACHING PROPOSAL

In 1982, New Jersey developed the first fast-track alternate route to teacher certification in the United States. Formally established in 1985, the program rested on the assumption that learning to teach is primarily a matter of on-the-job learning and training, since the practice of teaching cannot be taught or learned outside the classroom (Cooperman & Klagholz, 1985). The alternate program aimed to recruit college graduates with strong subject matter knowledge and then provide them with an intense summer program before they entered the classroom in the fall, as teachers of record.

The 200-hour program would cover core issues of teaching (e.g., class management and student learning). The teacher candidate was responsible for securing a job offer from a school (Cooperman, Webb, & Klagholz, 1983). Once the candidate found a job and passed screening by the district and school, she or he would receive a one-year provisional teaching license.

During that year, the teacher would be supported and regularly monitored by a mentor teacher and school principal. In order to receive a standard license, the teacher had to pass the National Teacher Exam, complete the 200-hour program, and earn a positive evaluation and endorsement by the school.

Reasons for Establishing the Program

The reasoning and motivations behind a public policy like establishing an alternate route to teaching are not always entirely clear. Sometimes policy makers express one set of reasons, while concealing or being unaware of other possibilities. This happened in the case of New Jersey.

The initial proposal laid out the rationale for the program in quite a stark language. According to the commissioner and his colleagues, New Jersey's teaching force was largely composed of academically deficient college students who had received poor teacher preparation. Cooperman and colleagues highlighted the lack of consensus regarding the professional knowledge taught in these programs. They questioned the need for theoretical foundations courses and pointed to the minimal standards required for graduation.

> For certification purposes, there is little basis for requiring specific theoretical courses. To do so would be merely to set up an artificial hurdle to professional access at a time when we can ill afford to turn away talented individuals. (Cooperman et al., 1983, 20)

Cooperman and his colleagues not only criticized teacher preparation, they challenged the legitimacy of teacher educators to serve as gatekeepers of the teaching profession. Furthermore, they implied that a teacher shortage exists and that the current teaching force is not as talented as those who would join teaching if teacher educators did not require them to go through their preparation programs.

> Those eligibility requirements [of traditional teacher preparation programs] were systematically attracting weak college students and failing to convert them into competent teachers. At the same time, they were screening out substantial numbers of talented men and women who wanted to teach and were capable of doing so. (Klagholz, 2000, 18)

The agenda and opinions of program officials dominated news coverage at the time. For example, a 1985 article in New Jersey's major newspaper, *Star-Ledger*, introduced the program in the following way:

> State education officials have launched a campaign to recruit new public school teachers from among recent graduates of the nation's most prestigious and selective colleges and universities. The effort has been made possible by the state's new "alternate route" certification procedure that allows school districts to hire graduates of traditional liberal arts programs as provisional teachers. The new teachers do not need to pursue conventional, college-based teacher training. Leo Klagholz, teacher certification director for the state education department, said the liberalized licensing approach makes New Jersey unique in the nation in its ability to compete with private preparatory schools in recruiting graduates from Ivy League and other highly selective schools. (Braun, 1985, 1 and 27)**[AQ: Should the extract have an ellipsis (two different pages cited in the source)?]**

Instead of relying on traditional teacher education programs, the alternate route architects argued that teachers should be proficient in their subject matter and hold a baccalaureate degree from an accredited college or university. Then they could learn practical teaching knowledge and skills on the job through an "internship," under the guidance of a qualified expert teacher who could assess them in accordance with established assessment criteria (Cooperman et al., 1983, 8–11; Klagholz, 2000, 15).

Cooperman and his colleagues boasted that the new alternate route and its requirements would improve the standards for entry into teaching. This would affect students in traditional teacher preparation programs as well as those majoring in any non-education field of study who would join teaching through the alternate route program.

The policy included a combination of untested assumptions and hopes, some legitimate, others questionable, which led to both positive and negative outcomes. With the approval of the alternate route program, the state determined that all teachers in New Jersey needed a bachelor's degree. Education would no longer count as an undergraduate major. Nor would the state grant emergency teaching certificates to individuals without a college degree. The latter decision was particularly important. The teaching profession has been plagued by this "backdoor entrance" which allows schools to offer temporary teaching jobs to candidates who do not meet minimum professional standards.

An important assumption was that teachers who know their subject well will be more effective than teachers whose education included a mix of content knowledge and generic pedagogy. The claim that majoring in one's teaching subject in college automatically provides needed knowledge and skills for teaching that subject sounded logical to Cooperman and his colleagues, despite the absence of supporting evidence. In fact, many researchers believe that teaching subject matter effectively depends on subject specific understandings of teaching, learning, students, and context, in addition to relevant subject matter knowledge (e.g., Ball, 1988).

The third requirement of the new plan involved a so-called year-long, mentored internship. This would "provide the appropriate vehicle for transmitting the applied knowledge and techniques which are related to effective teaching and which undergird the profession" (Cooperman et al., 1983, 10). Advocates added that teaching internships should not only be required for the new alternate route teachers, but should also be integrated into traditional, university-based teacher preparation (10).

After a short summer of preparation, the alternate route provided each new teacher with a mentor who was supposed to provide advice and feedback during the teachers' first year on the job. Mentors were also responsible for evaluating alternate route teachers. These characteristics make New Jersey's alternate route the first "fast-track" alternate route, predating and most likely inspiring Teach For America and similar programs which rest on similar assumptions and embrace the model of brief preparation and thin support.

Many teacher educators oppose this model. They argue that teacher education programs should provide a true internship in which teacher candidates serve as apprentices in an experienced (mentor) teacher's classroom, gradually assuming more responsibilities as the year progresses and only taking full responsibility as teachers of record after a full year of professional study and guided practice. In this model, the internship is part of the preparation phase. The following year, when the teacher becomes the official teacher of record, she or he would also be assigned a school-based mentor.[4]

Beyond the debate over program features and requirements which the alternate route pushed to the fore, the first alternate route program made other unproven claims. Take, for instance, the claim that the alternate route program would attract the best and brightest students. Klagholz (2000) asserted that alternate route teachers received better scores on the National Teacher Examination compared to traditional route teachers. While his numbers support the claim, the differences were usually small (e.g., biology 660 vs. 641; 663 v. 657 for elementary teachers). Moreover no statistical tests were used to measure the significance of the differences between the two groups.[5]

Another open question concerns the supply and demand of teachers before and after the alternate route. While New Jersey officials claimed that there was a shortage of qualified teachers, they never offered clear evidence. Klagholz's argument that alternate route graduates were eventually hired by schools offers some weak support at best, because it does not prove the existence of a shortage. Moreover, we know that many alternate route teachers went in disproportionally large numbers to private schools where they did not need teacher certification to begin with (Klagholz, 2000). It seems likely that the teacher shortage argument was used as an excuse to garner more legitimacy for a program that was ideologically driven by a neo-liberal agenda and mission to improve the quality of teachers.

In sum, the program planners in New Jersey sought to improve the quality of teachers by offering what they deemed a better alternative to traditional teacher preparation in colleges and universities. In the process, they sought to challenge and circumvent the long-standing professional authority and monopoly of what they saw as failing teacher preparation programs (Cooperman & Klagholz, 1985).

CONCLUSIONS

This chapter traces the motivations and reasoning behind the foundation of New Jersey's alternate route to teacher certification, including the immediate and larger political contexts which framed and shaped these motivations. Underlying the debate over the alternate route were two distinct worldviews held by different professional groups—teacher educators and teacher unions, on the one hand, and a coalition of neo-liberal government politicians, policy makers, academics, and businessmen/women on the other. For these two camps, the debate revolved largely around ideological issues of power and control over the teaching profession.

In the case of New Jersey, teacher educators and teachers' unions believed in and fought to preserve the status quo in which colleges, schools, and departments of education largely controlled the supply of teachers by serving as gatekeepers for the profession and by recommending to state officials those candidates who met minimal professional requirements for licensure. These two groups also insisted that they were best equipped to control and dictate the type of knowledge, skills, and dispositions necessary for beginning teachers. The neo-liberal coalition, led by New Jersey's newly elected governor and the state department of education, challenged these two core professional prerogatives, arguing that they were unjustly held by self-serving professional groups who betrayed the public and were only trying to defend their perks.

The coalition of challengers further argued that the public would be better off if the state broke the gatekeeping grip of the profession over the supply of teachers by opening a competing, state-sponsored alternate route to teaching and by changing the composition of content knowledge required not only by beginning teachers in the state-sponsored alternate route, but also by teacher candidates in traditional teacher education programs. This meant eliminating the education major in colleges and universities, replacing it with an education minor, and requiring teacher candidates to have an extensive internship.

Policy makers in New Jersey based their support for establishing the state-sponsored alternate route in their commitment to neo-liberal ideological principles. Looking back on his flagship policy fifteen years later, Klagholz (2000), one of the main architects of the alternate route, could not point to any substantial evidence to justify this radical experiment which he so vehemently supported.

This is not to say that alternate routes are unimportant or represent a failed experiment. Rather, these programs have been a catalyzing force for important debates in the field. They have also challenged old guard teacher educators to face important claims and criticism about the accreditation of programs, the knowledge base and dispositions of teachers, and the quality of candidates being recruited and prepared by teacher education programs.

Since the inception of the New Jersey program, alternate routes programs in the United States have not only mushroomed, but also evolved in terms of their structure and mission. While some alternate route programs, particularly Teach For America, have remained close to the original model advanced by New Jersey,[6] more and more teacher preparation programs combine elements from both traditional and alternate route programs. As a result, the divide between new, alternate routes and programs based at colleges and universities has largely disappeared.

Fast-track alternate route programs like the New Jersey program and Teach For America use teacher education programs at colleges and universities to prepare their students and grant them M.A. degrees. There are also examples of hybrid programs which have adopted from alternate route programs a more targeted and selective recruitment policy and a substantial internship experience, while taking from traditional preparation programs a focus on pedagogy, school contexts, and serious mentoring of teacher candidates (Feiman-Nemser, Tamir, & Hammerness, 2014).

In sum, while the creation of the first alternate route program in New Jersey was never fully justified on purely educational ground, it has been widely influential. On the positive side, it promoted extensive discussions about teacher quality, advanced research, and stimulated improvements in teacher preparation.

Fast-track programs, like Teach For America, polarized debates in teacher education between those who advocated recruiting smart candidates and those who placed their bets on serious preparation. Similarly, fast-track programs further politicized debates over future reforms in teaching, learning, and public schooling. Take for example the bitter struggles of teachers' unions with the coalition of so-called reform entrepreneurs, policy elites, and philanthropists, whose support for alternate routes was part of a wider effort to replace public schools with charter schools, revamp teacher evaluations, establish competitive pay, and ultimately abolish teacher tenure.

Despite the gap between the big promises and modest changes, alternate route programs have had some positive intended consequences. They injected new blood into teaching by recruiting motivated young and second-career teachers and may be partly responsible for general changes in the population of teachers, which increasingly includes teacher of ethnic minority background and stronger academic credentials, particularly in urban metropolitan areas.[7]

The proliferation of alternate routes and their emphasis on real-life classroom experience facilitated an important debate between teacher educators who believe in the importance of providing prospective teachers a broad theoretical background through university courses and those who believe that teaching is best learned through extensive, clinical experience.

Finally, the creation of alternate routes promoted competition among programs, which in turn increased scrutiny and led to more research and evaluation by states, organizations, and accreditation bodies, independent teacher education programs, and educational researchers at large. Some of the areas that benefited the most have been research on teacher recruitment, preparation, and retention, as well as research on teacher assessment and teacher quality, including the controversial strategy of using value added measures to evaluate teacher education programs and teacher performance.

NOTES

1. I say presumably, because studies have shown that standardized tests have a history of intentional systematic discrimination against African American teachers under the guise of a universal meritocratic test (Sedlak, 2008). Moreover, large-scale studies have repeatedly failed to show a clear link between teacher effectiveness and teacher grades on standardized tests and/or certification (e.g., Wilson, 2009).

2. Although the ideas of vouchers and charters did not come to fruition during the Reagan administration (1981–1989), states started adopting them in the early 1990s.

3. See Tamir (2008) for a more elaborated version of this story.

4. For a detailed description of alternate route case studies of fast track and gradual track teacher education programs, which discusses the interaction between preparation and internship and their contribution to beginning teachers' effectiveness, see, Inspiring teaching, preparing teacher to succeed in mission driven schools (Feiman-Nemser, Tamir, & Hammerness 2014).

5. A table with teacher scores appears in Klagholz (2000, 15). The document is available at http://edex.s3-us-west-2.amazonaws.com/publication/pdfs/klagholz_7.pdf.

6. It is probably not by chance that Teach For America was established in Princeton, New Jersey, a few years after the state-sponsored program was launched at Trenton (15-minute drive from Princeton). Thus, structurally and content-wise, Wendy Kopp's program was hardly new at the time. Yet Kopp's commitment and resolve to build an alternate route to teaching that went beyond state lines and country borders, recruited heavily and efficiently at Ivy League colleges and drew substantial funding and support from private funders, elevated Teach For America to prominence.

7. At this point this is no more than a hypothesis that requires a careful analysis, but there are multiple case studies suggesting that some alternate routes have been indeed pushing hard to recruit students with minority and/or high academic ability backgrounds.

REFERENCES

Abbott, A. (1988). *The system of professions: An essay on the division of expert labor*. Chicago, IL: University of Chicago Press.

Ball, D. L. (1988). *Research on teaching mathematics: Making subject matter knowledge part of the equation*. Research report 88-2. National Center for Research on Teacher Education. Michigan State University, East Lansing, Michigan.

Braun, R. J. (1985). State recruits teachers at prestigious colleges. (Newark) *Star-Ledger*, May 19, 1–27.

Cooperman, S., & Klagholz, L. (1985). New Jersey's alternative route to certification. *Phi Delta Kappan 66*(10), 691–695.

Cooperman, S., Webb, A., & Klagholz, L. (1983). *An alternative route to teacher selection and professional quality assurance*. Trenton: New Jersey State Department of Education.

Klagholz, Leo. (2000). *Growing better teachers in the garden state: New Jersey's "alternate route" to teacher certification*. Washington, DC: Thomas B. Fordham Foundation.

National Commission on Excellence in Education. (1983). *A nation at risk: The imperative for educational reform*. Washington, DC: U.S. Department of Education.

Salmore, B. G., & Salmore, S. A. (1993). *New Jersey politics and government: Suburban politics comes of age*. Lincoln: University of Nebraska Press.

Tamir, E. (2008). Theorizing the politics of educational reform: The case of New Jersey's alternate route to teacher certification. *American Journal of Education, 115*(1), 65–95.

Chapter Two

The Impact of Alternative Routes on the Work and Identities of Teacher Educators

The English Case

Jean Murray, Gerry Czerniawski, and Warren Kidd

Pre-service routes in England now exist within a fragmented and diversifying teacher education system. There are many ways to become a teacher, including alternative, employment-based routes. These routes exist alongside and sometimes interwoven with traditional study at degree or post-graduate levels. This chapter traces the development of the pre-service system, emphasizing its politicization since 1984 and exploring the concept of "partnership."

The main focus is the controversial School Direct program. In existence since 2010, School Direct is an employment-based route in which schools recruit intending teachers, provide most of their school experience, and arrange any other training required for qualified teacher status. This route has brought a new cohort of school-based teacher educators into teacher education, which has consequences for the traditional occupational group of Higher Education (HE)-based teacher educators. The chapter draws on two small-scale studies which shed light on how school-based and HE-based teacher educators are operating in the rapidly changing and diversifying contexts of initial teacher preparation in England.

CONTEXT

With a teacher workforce of approximately half a million teachers, pre-service teacher education (ITE) operates on a considerable scale. The numbers of student teachers (often called "trainees") in 2015/16 was expected to be around 35,000. The supply, recruitment, and retention of teachers, especially during periods of national economic prosperity when new graduates are less likely to enter teaching, have long been key government concerns. These issues and the politicized nature of the field of ITE have contributed to the evolution of alternative routes in England and to changing roles for teacher educators in both universities and schools.

Since 1984, ITE has been subjected to repeated government-sponsored interventions as part of an ongoing effort to raise educational standards in schools. Cumulatively, these interventions have changed the language, cultures, governance, regulatory structures, and institutional organization of ITE, making it more school-focused and instrumental and centered on the "practical" knowledge of teaching (Murray & Mutton, 2015).

With a growing emphasis on the practicum and experiential knowledge, all programs now include large amounts of time in school. Post-graduate student teachers, for example, spend at least twenty-four weeks of their thirty-six-week program in schools; undergraduate degree program typically include the same amount of time in school, if not more. On school-based routes, the amount of training time spent in school can be 100%.

As a result of these changes, ITE has moved away from the dominance of the Higher Education Institutions and toward schools as far more influential stakeholders. Since government legislation in 1984 set up the initial requirements for schools and universities to work more closely together, the concept of "partnership" has been central. Further legislation in the early 1990s required that all pre-service programs be planned, taught, and assessed "in partnership" between schools and universities. By 2000, a continuum of partnership models had emerged, ranging from university-led partnership with schools to entirely school-led schemes (Furlong, Barton, Miles, Whiting, & Whitly, 2000).

Under many partnership arrangements, high education–based (HE) teacher educators experienced a reduction in the amount of time they spent supervising the practicum—meaning observing and assessing pre-service teachers in schools. Experienced teachers, usually called "mentors," took over many of these functions. This, in turn, led to new roles for HE-based teacher educators as supporters and managers of partnerships. Large numbers of teacher educators and mentors engaged in boundary-crossing activities. Teacher educators helped mentors guide pre-service teachers' learning during the practicum and carry out formative and summative assessments of their teaching.

At their best, these pedagogies enabled mentor teachers to understand the learning needs and patterns of student teachers. They also relied on a strong sense of trust, shared values, and the exchange of difference expertise by all parties involved in pre-service education. These pedagogies also had the potential to generate collaborative learning opportunities for both mentors and HE-based teacher educators, working together outside the traditional epistemological boundaries of schools and universities.

In the 1990s, some forms of partnership activities in England created "hybrid spaces" (Zeichner, 2010). Such spaces enabled the development of research-informed clinical practice in teacher education.[1] Yet despite some positive examples and the length of time during which school-university partnerships were mandated, some partnership arrangements did not take full advantage of the contributions that universities and their teacher educators could make to the learning of pre-service students (McNamara and Murray, 2013, 17).

Alternative Routes: History and Growth

Alternative routes into teaching have a relatively long history in England, prompted by teacher shortages during times of economic prosperity. Another factor, particularly during the New Labour government of 1997–2010, was the desire to diversify the workforce. Government targets included bringing more men into primary (elementary) school teaching and increasing the number of teachers from Black and minority ethnic groups.

The Licensed and Articled Teacher Schemes established in 1989 as school-based, alternative routes enabled university graduates to become teachers without following a post-graduate program. School-centered ITT schemes in which schools take responsibility for ITT programs began in the 1990s. These routes could be implemented without the sustained involvement of universities. In fact, relatively few student teachers participated in such programs during 1990s (Furlong et al., 2000), so their influence was limited, although their symbolic importance was high.

The Graduate Teacher Program, originally aimed at mature graduates who did not want to undertake a traditional university course, was launched in the late 1990s. It increased the numbers studying on alternative routes. Although successful, the scheme was eventually replaced by the School Direct program.

In 2010, the incoming coalition government made wide-ranging changes to schooling. This included the implementation of Free Schools, independent, state-funded schools that can be set up by parents, religious bodies, and charities, and the acceleration of the academies program which are state-funded schools free of local authority control and sometimes managed by "chains" of co-sponsors. The government also expressed dissatisfaction with the quality of ITE and skepticism about the role of the university. Teaching was positioned as a basic "craft," involving limited knowledge beyond a subject-specialist degree.

At the center of these latest interventions were new school-led models of training, designed to open up the "market" of ITE to new "providers." Now many such providers offer diverse "alternative" routes into teaching. These alternative routes exist alongside traditional study for the one-year, post-graduate program or undergraduate degrees that lead to qualified teacher status.

There are also schemes aimed at particular groups such as Teach First, similar to the Teach For America program, which recruits candidates with "good" undergraduate degrees, and Troops into Teaching for ex-members of the armed forces. An "assessment only" route allows intending teachers to apply for qualification through assessment against the eight current Teacher Standards. Free schools and academies are now permitted to recruit and employ untrained teachers if they wish, although all other state-funded schools still have to employ trained teachers.

Since 2010, the main instrument of the pre-service reforms has been the employment-based route called School Direct. Schools can opt for their trainees to obtain a basic qualification through school-based training only or for trainees to work with another provider to follow a program leading to a post-graduate award. Currently the scheme accounts for 25% of all ITE places.

The scale and speed of this growth took the university sector by surprise. Many universities were hit hard by the swift introduction of School Direct and the accompanying cuts in their allocated pre-service numbers. A number of small, subject-specific secondary programs were closed, some HE-based teacher educators were made redundant, and many commentators feared for the ongoing viability of other HE provision.

In order to protect their surviving programs in this new ITE market, many universities relied on securing training contracts from schools under the School Direct scheme. In this market-based model, the customer, in this case the school, purchases an ITE program from a "service provider" (not neces-sarily a university), sometimes through a process of competitive tendering. Pre-service training in England now exists within a fast-changing, fragment-ed and diversifying system with multiple providers and diverse routes into teaching existing alongside and sometimes interwoven with traditional study at degree or post-graduate levels.

According to Whitty (2014), this fragmented context is a result of the "neo-liberal combination of the strong state and the free market" (471). Cer-tainly, the idea that universities make a distinctive and necessary contribution to ITE has been steadily eroded. In particular, the increasing emphasis on alternative, school-based routes has had significant implications for teacher educators as an occupational group and for their changing roles.

Teacher Educators: Changing Definitions, Roles, and Responsibilities

These changes have dramatically enlarged the occupational group of teacher educators. Only a decade ago, in England as in many other countries, teacher educators were employed by universities on full- or part-time contracts. That HE-based occupational group has now been joined by various types of school-based teacher educators.

In particular, the School Direct route has brought a new cohort of educators into teacher education. In addition to mentoring roles which have existed to support the practicum since the early 1990s, school-based teacher educators now take on responsibility for organizing all aspects of ITE, including the recruitment, design, and implementation of programs as well as assessment of candidates at the end of the training process. Most of these educators also teach or mentor pre-service teachers within the school workplace. Depending on the type of training route offered in their schools, these school-based teacher educators sometimes work alongside HE-based teacher educators.

One study of this emerging occupational group looked at 23 school-based teacher educators working in six schools (Czerniawski, Kidd, & Murray, 2013). The sample consisted of senior school staff responsible for coordinating, implementing, and developing all the ITE provisions in the schools, and subject specialists, often less experienced teachers, responsible for inducting individual trainees into the school, guiding and mentoring their progress, observing teaching and giving feedback, and finally assessing. All of these school-based teacher educators worked on both traditional post-graduate and School Direct programs in partnership with a university.

The researchers used semi-structured, face-to-face interviews to capture individuals' understanding of their identities and knowledge as both teachers and teacher educators, and their perceptions of university-based teacher educators. The interviews were transcribed and subjected to open coding, which generated a number of themes. The codes were then refined by repeated analysis in order to identify recurring themes and core categories.

The study offers numerous examples of new practices growing out of previous ways of working. The school-based teacher educators showed considerable confidence in their knowledge, experience, and skills. They saw themselves playing crucial roles in the professional development of trainees through their ability to "lead the teacher to a place where they can solve their own problems and find their own solutions, where they can think through issues themselves." They regarded themselves as "guides" and "good practitioners," engaged in "modeling classroom skills and best practice'" for and with their student teachers. Other practices included "developing enquiry and critical thinking skills about teaching," encouraging students to "question dominant ideas and practices," and supporting "reflection and using it to develop practical theory."

In order to teach and mentor trainees, the school-based teacher educators saw themselves and their colleagues as needing "commitments to reflective practice," ongoing interest in "the debate about teaching and learning" and "flexibility." One person agreed that the latter was important since educators should not be "stuck in their own comfort zones." These school-based teacher educators rightly claimed and celebrated their expertise, knowledge, and pedagogical skills in teaching teachers. They also saw that their knowledge base of school teaching was significantly enhanced by their roles as teacher educators.

> I get my knowledge of classroom practice by being in it, from the new ideas coming into the school through government policy and by my ability to explore with my trainee a sense of "why" we do things.

This educator's developing identity and practice as a school-based teacher educator were formed by a synergistic process, centered on her own developing knowledge of school teaching and further enhanced through the collaborative learning that took place while she mentored student teachers.

The most experienced educators in the study sought legitimacy for their knowledge base by referencing the variety and depth of experiences they had had as teachers working in a number of different schools. They saw this as important because they were training pre-service teachers to work in many different situations. Variety and depth of personal knowledge enabled them to offer "alternative ways of doing things." One senior school-based teacher educator noted:

> I've taught in six schools. If you've only worked in one school you either spend your whole time critiquing it or believe that this is the only way of doing things. It is therefore essential to have been in more than one school.

Less experienced school-based teacher educators thought their *recent* qualification as teachers gave them skills and knowledge which they could bring to their trainees. "Familiarity with being mentored myself" contributed to their senses that they empathize, understand and identify with student teachers.

New, hybrid ways of working were being forged through School Direct. These were based on the school-based teacher educators' sense of confidence in their professional credentials and authority to engage in teacher education work. Those new practices and enhanced sense of confidence had also developed from the schools' previous partnerships with the university.

The more traditional group of HE-teacher educators have also seen considerable changes in their work, roles, and identities as alternative pre-service routes have proliferated. Some traditional roles have been eroded and replaced by other work. Many teacher educators now spend less time supervising and assessing practicum students and more time managing partnerships with schools. Increased levels of bureaucracy in ITE and in universities has meant that educators now manage audit and performance measures for their student teachers and themselves.

Many Schools of Education were ambivalent about supporting research on the part of some teacher educators, particularly those without conventional research profiles. As a result, engagement in research by teacher educators became more limited in some higher education institutions (HEIs), increasing their sense of marginalization. Finally, there has been a growing emphasis on recent and relevant knowledge of schooling. This knowledge was prioritized in recruitment and monitored during inspections.

Experiential knowledge of schooling and identities as "once a teacher" often formed the foundations of pedagogy for many teacher educators (Murray, 2014). The knowledge and pedagogical skills of teacher education itself (Murray, 2002) or knowledge of teaching teachers (Loughran, 2006) was often under-valued or unrecognized. By 2010 then, HE-based teacher educators had already experienced multiple changes in their roles and identities, but further changes were to come through subsequent ITE reforms.

As School Direct became the dominant route into teaching, the authors of this chapter conducted a second study, this time of HE-based teacher education. As the number of pre-service teacher places allocated directly to universities reduced sharply, each institution had to secure training contracts for as many trainees as possible in order to keep their post-graduate College of Education (PGCE) programs viable. At the same time, the schools which had been allocated School Direct places had to recruit their own trainees, decide what training program to offer, including whether to draw support from a university or another designated "provider" and whether to ask their trainees to gain a post-graduate certificate or qualified teacher status only.

Many schools decided to work with universities and to ask their trainees to complete the post-graduate programs those institutions offered. But schools were explicitly advised by the National College of Teaching and Leadership, an organization that regulates ITE, to ascertain carefully what particular universities might offer in terms of recruitment, curriculum provision, and assessment—and at what price. Many schools, particularly those in dense urban areas with a number of universities close by, followed the government's market model and "shopped around" for their training programs; many such schools became "smart shoppers," conducting their negotiations with a shrew eye for the program offering best value.

The researchers attempted to discover what kinds of work HE-based teacher educators were doing in these rapidly changing contexts of the School Direct route and whether this was new and different work or an extension of previous work patterns. The study, which involved a sample of fifty-seven teacher educators based in nine universities in England, used online, open-ended questionnaires and semi-structured interviews. The study found that School Direct had brought about a number of changes. Teacher educators engaged in "selling" their courses to schools. Some shared recruitment practices between schools and universities emerged. Some teacher educators experienced a marginalization of their expertise, as curriculum and assessment practices were revised to accommodate school requirements and extended forms of pedagogies which guided mentors emerged.

As the market-led model swung into action and schools became "smart shoppers," some teacher educators invested a great deal of time generating and securing training contracts. This was especially true for senior teacher educators (especially those in charge of post-graduate programs) and partnership managers. These teacher educators were often doing what one interviewee described as "selling and marketing" their programs in schools. This often meant undertaking detailed financial negotiations around the business model on offer and deciding exactly how much the university would charge the school for the program. In this highly competitive process, much of this work took place outside the university in schools. As one person said,

> I spend much more time in schools talking about our School Direct offer and how schools might get involved. I've become a salesperson trying to attract customers and outbid other local providers, whilst still maintaining the long established close relationships we have with our local colleagues.

Another added, "I have become a skilled negotiator and diplomat. With my new financial negotiation skills, I can give schools a very detailed breakdown of what £9,000[2] buys at our university." These university-based teacher educators found that they needed to take on new roles and acquire new skills, more akin to consultancy, marketing, and sales work on behalf of their universities. For many, these were unwelcome roles, as one person wrote, "I came into Higher Education to teach teachers, not to be a salesman!"

Another changing aspect involved new recruitment practices. Since the early 1990s under partnership arrangements between schools and universities, teachers often served on interview panels alongside HE-based educators, helping to evaluate the suitability of prospective teacher candidates. Still, the university managed the recruitment procedures, assuming major responsibility for the interview and selection process.

School Direct changed those processes. Now schools recruited and selected their own teacher candidates. Some schools chose to do this alone; others asked for support from the university, particularly during selection interviews. Some of the HE-based teacher educators in the study talked about sitting on panels dominated by school staff and participating in interviews held in schools. Here is how one interviewee described these joint recruitment practices.

> School XX[3] was interviewing for two School Direct places in Biology and Chemistry so all the candidates were asked to teach a lesson in their subject, with me and two school staff observing them. . . . Given that they had no previous teaching experience, I thought they did very well, but the school staff were not impressed because none of them included any element of assessment for learning in the lessons.

The HE-based educator was impressed by the six candidates and would have recruited them to the post-graduate certificate because all had "training potential." The school staff initially wanted to reject them because of the quality of the teaching they had observed. The teacher educator thought the school's expectations of these inexperienced candidates were unrealistically high. After lengthy discussion, the teacher educator managed to persuade his school colleagues that two of the candidates had real potential and, with the necessary support, could develop into excellent teachers within the school.

In this case, the school eventually recognized and accepted the teacher educator's knowledge of pre-service teachers' potential and development and appointed the two candidates. But the teacher educators also had to be flexible and empathetic. Working together, school staff and teacher educators were able to recruit two strong candidates, a good outcome for all.

Other examples of changing recruitment practices were less positive, indicating how power shifts within ITE gave far more autonomy and power to schools. One HE-based educator recounted that

> When school XX was recruiting with us (her university) for a School Direct trainee in physics, the interview panel consisted of me, the head teacher, the head of subject and the year tutor. There were four candidates, three of whom had degrees in the subject so they are like gold dust. I would have recruited all three of them for the post-graduate program at the university. One of them was particularly outstanding.

After four interviews and much panel discussion, the school decided not to accept her preferred candidate but to select instead a candidate with a degree in Biology but "only an A level[4] in physics and little other subject knowledge." This candidate was a mature person making a career-change and the school staff felt that he would fit in, despite his apparent lack of degree-level subject knowledge.

In this case, the teacher educator felt that her previous "gatekeeping" experience and guidance were "marginalized" and the subject knowledge imperatives she felt were important in teaching were over-ridden by the school's preference. She did not feel "in control of the process" and had been "relegated to the role of ignored recruitment consultant." In this and similar examples, a clear power shift reduced HE-teacher educators' traditional gate-keeping responsibilities. Overall, the study revealed considerable divergence in recruitment practices, with many shared practices emerging but also some perceived marginalization of HE expertise.

Another recurring theme in the study was requests from schools for re-vised curricula and assessment procedures. For example, one school re-quested that the post-graduate course for their School Direct trainees should be amended to include "substantial coverage of behavior management, teach-ing English as a second language, creativity and teaching in faith schools." The school wanted all three topics covered in depth and tailored to the specific pupils and the ways in which they were being taught. Other schools requested amendments to reflect their particular approaches to pupil learning. One school, part of a large chain of academies, stated that "their 'trainees needed to learn how to teach in the XX Academy way."

Schools also asked for new forms of trainee assessment. For example, a group of schools wanted trainees to pass a written assignment on behavior management techniques. In some cases, schools challenged assessment deci-sions of HE-based teacher educators, seeking to "get rid of students *(train-ees)* they saw as poor or who didn't fit into the school quickly without giving a chance for learning how to teach to take place."

In negotiating these changes around curricula and assessment, the HE-based educators had to work with their school-based counterparts who were responsible for the School Direct program. They described themselves as "drawing on but adjusting" their previous knowledge and experience in order to "mediate with the schools and reach consensus."

CONCLUSION

Despite their small scale, the research reported here sheds light on how school-based and HE-based teacher educators are being affected by the di-versifying contexts of teacher education in England. Within the highly regu-lated and politicized context of ITE in England, increasing emphases on partnerships and on alternative, school-led and school-based routes to teach-ing have had significant, long-term implications for teacher educators as an occupational group. Underway since 1984, these changes have accelerated in the twenty-first century. In particular, the introduction at scale of School Direct has had significant and long-lasting effects for all teacher educators in England.

A new occupational sub-group of school-based teacher educators has emerged with growing confidence in their "second order knowledge, skills and expertise: in working with student teachers" (Murray, 2002). These educators rightly claim and celebrate their new hybrid roles and practices as they work simultaneously as classroom teachers and school-based teacher educators, contributing new and valuable voices to teacher education.

The work of some HE-based teacher educators has been re-framed as consultancy, marketing, and sales work on behalf of their higher education institutions (HEIs). Other teacher educators are extending their previous practices based on past work with partnership schools. These practices include serving as brokers between schools and their HEIs to support student teacher learning (Lunenberg, Korthagen, & Dengerink, 2013), operating in "hybrid" spaces located between schools and universities, and developing extensive pedagogies for working with school-based teacher educators.

Some of these practices seem problematic, especially when they result in narrow and instrumental forms of ITE, constructed around strong local knowledge uninformed by research. These are worrying trends leading to less critical, theoretically relevant forms of teacher education. It is also worrisome that some new practices ignore the accumulated experience and expertise of HE-based teacher educators—expertise which the system can ill-afford to lose. HE-based teacher educators, particularly those involved in sales and marketing work, run the risk of generating yet more bureaucracy in an already over-stretched and over-regulated teacher education system.

Still, from the reconfigured spaces of teacher education, new practices are emerging, grounded in shared expertise and new forms of distributed knowledge. As the landscape of teacher education shifts, it is possible that through a re-drawing of past partnership boundaries and practices, a movement toward the development of a critical pedagogy of teacher education may result (McNamara & Murray, 2013, 23). It is critical that these new ways of operating center not on competition and difference among stakeholders, but on communal efforts to improve the quality of student teacher learning—and subsequently, the quality of pupils' achievements as learners.

NOTES

1. The term "research-informed clinical practice" is variously defined, but the term fundamentally implies bringing research-based understandings of teaching and learning into dialogue with the developing professional understandings of student teachers (Burns & Mutton, 2013).

2. £9,000 is currently the fee charged by most English universities for a year of postgraduate study.

3. The names of all the institutions in this study have been removed to protect teacher educator and school anonymity.

4. "A" or "Advanced level" qualifications are taken at the age of 18 in England and often form the basis for admission to university.

REFERENCES

Czerniawski, G., Kidd, W., & Murray, J. (2013). *Understanding teacher educators as teachers of teachers: Exploring multiple perspectives.* Paper presented at the AERA Conference, San Francisco, May 1.

Furlong, J., Barton, L., Miles, S., Whiting, C., & Whitty, G. (2000). *Teacher education in transition: Reforming professionalism?* Buckingham: Open University Press.

Loughran, J. (2006). *Developing a pedagogy of teacher education.* London: Falmer.

Lunenberg, M., Korthagen, F., & Dengerink, J. (2013). *Six roles of teacher educators: A review study on the profession of teacher educator.* Paper presented at the AERA Conference, San Francisco, May 1.

McNamara, O., & Murray, J. (2013). *The School Direct Program and Its Implications*, York: Higher Education Academy.

Murray, J. (2002). Between the chalkface and the ivory towers? A study of the professionalism of teacher educators. *Collected Original Resources in Education, 26*(3), 1–530.

Murray, J. (2014). Teacher educators' constructions of professionalism: Change and diversity in teacher education. *Asia Pacific Journal of Teacher Education, 42*(1), 7–21.

Murray, J., & Mutton, T. (2016). Teacher education in England: Change in abundance, continuities in question. In *Teacher education in times of change* (pp. 57–74). Bristol: Policy Press.

Whitty, G. (2014). Recent developments in teacher training and their consequences for the "University Project" in education. *Oxford Review of Education, 4*(4), 466–481.

Zeichner, K. (2010). Rethinking the connections between campus courses and field experiences in college-and university-based teacher education. *Journal of Teacher Education, 61*(1–2), 89–99.

Chapter Three

The Case of Hotam Naomi

More Than a Teacher Education Program

Michal Shani, Sara Shadmi-Wortman,
and Edith Tabak

Hotam Naomi is an innovative, alternative teacher education program in Israel which trains teachers as activist leaders of change through education. The program developed through a collaborative partnership among two established Colleges of Education, Levinsky and Oranim, and the Hotam organization. This chapter describes the first year of collaboration (2014–2015), a year of constructing professional wisdom in teacher education through partnership and enquiry.

HOTAM'S SOCIO-POLITICAL AND IDEOLOGICAL ROOTS

Zeichner and Pea-Sandoval (2015) identify three major positions in debates about teacher education in the United States: defenders, reformers, and transformers. Defenders call for greater investment in the current system, but see no need for significant changes. Reformers argue that schools of education have failed to fulfill their mission and current teacher education programs must be uprooted and replaced. Transformers call for major changes in the current system, increasing effectiveness by relating coursework to the realities and complexities of schools.

Situated in the transformer camp, Hotam, or Teach First Israel (TFI), offers its own unique response and stance to the current debates in teacher education. With government support, it concentrates on building up the teaching profession within Israel by preparing high-quality teachers who serve as activist leaders and bridge the achievement gap by teaching in the geographical periphery and working on the social periphery.

ORGANIZATIONAL BACKGROUND AND HISTORY

Hotam was launched in 2010 in partnership with the Joint Distribution Committee (JDC), the Ministry of Education, Ha-Kol Hinuch Movement, and the Naomi Foundation. Its mission is to address system-based inequality in education by recruiting and training the country's brightest college graduates to teach in the weakest schools in the social and geographic periphery.

Hotam seeks to cultivate leaders who will use the education system to direct children from disadvantaged backgrounds toward positive life trajectories. The program accepts candidates with leadership qualities who are deeply motivated to engage in education and to play a significant role in social change. These university and college graduates come from different academic backgrounds including mathematics, science, English, Bible, literacy, and history. Most are or have been involved in voluntary social activities, which reflect their mission to support people and to promote the practices of social justice.

During the admissions process, candidates participate in personal interviews and group meetings. In conversations about how to improve schools, they must display open-mindedness, a willingness to learn, curiosity toward different mindsets and people, and an ability to withstand a high level of uncertainty. They must also demonstrate a passion to act and make a difference in the future of disadvantaged children.

Those who are accepted to the program are assigned to carefully chosen schools in Israel's geographical and social periphery. Candidates receive five weeks of summer training in a residential school managed by the partnership of Hotam, Levinsky, and Oranim. After these five weeks, candidates start working at their pre-assigned schools as teachers, while continuing their teacher preparation at Levinsky College of Education one day a week for a full year.

Hotam teachers receive ongoing supervision and mentoring throughout their training while they study toward their teaching certificate. Some need to fulfill academic requirements in their subject matter area. In such cases, a personal program that meets the educational academic standards is developed.

The Hotam organization stipulates that teachers must be mentored throughout their entire career in response to changes in the system and their changing roles. Hotam teachers have a school-based mentor and a district guide from the Hotam organization who offer counseling and educational support at each career stage, from initial teacher preparation and induction to ongoing professional development.

Hotam alumni are considered the program's ambassadors. They form a community with a shared vision and mission to spread the Hotam ideology. Some alumni spread Hotam's ideas by becoming part of the Hotam staff, taking positions as mentors in school, regional leaders, and so on.

The Hotam Naomi training program was initially led by two academic organizations—Beit Berl Teacher Education College and Haifa University (2010–2014). Under their auspices, the program met the requirements for teacher training of university graduates (Grinfeld & Barlev, 2013).

In 2014, a new call was issued inviting teacher education schools and universities to collaborate with Hotam in developing of a new teacher education program. The Levinsky and Oranim Colleges of Education saw this as an opportunity to challenge the current teacher education program. This chapter focuses on the first year of the Hotam Naomi teacher education program under the new partnership between the Levinsky and Oranim Colleges of Education and the Hotam organization.

VISION AND PRINCIPLES

With a common agreement in hand, all the parties assumed that a new program would emerge through mutual dialogue among educators. Each college chose an academic leader, an experienced teacher educator and activist in teacher education, schooling, and social affairs. The first task was to design a program addressing critiques of similar programs around the world and taking into account the distinctive features of Hotam program and Hotam teachers.

Hotam teachers are young men and women with high levels of self-awareness, expectations, and commitment. Ambitious and idealistic, they have strong academic backgrounds in different areas. Hotam teachers work in schools with a high rate of poor, underprivileged, and at-risk students. Their training consists of five weeks of intensive training during the summer, after which they enter almost full-time teaching (80% full-time equivalency) in elementary, middle, or high schools with all the responsibilities of teaching various subjects, managing classrooms, and working with high-needs students. During their first year of teaching the Hotamists continue the training program one day a week in the teacher education college.

The two academic leaders outlined an academic program based on the following principles:

- The need to develop a comprehensive understanding of students and communities, including a nuanced understandings of intergroup and intra-group diversity;
- Leadership and activism by viewing the school in the context of the community and the larger society;
- Learning from practice under the mentorship of experienced teacher educators and through the integration of practice and theory;
- Creating a community of educators as the main platform for leading social change in schools and communities;
- Aspiring to academic excellence, outstanding teaching, and accountability.

CONFLICTS AND TENSIONS

These principles aligned with the Ariav Report (Ministry of Education, 2006), the current mandatory guidelines for teacher education programs in Israel established by the Ministry of Education. The Ariav paradigm, aimed at promoting a new vision of teacher professionalism, reflects a commitment to inquiry and lifelong learning. It encourages connections between theory and practice, integration among different parts of the professional curriculum and a deepening of disciplinary and pedagogical knowledge. It depends on collaboration with schools.

The complex context of the Hotam program and the current dissatisfaction with the outcomes of teacher education called for creative and innovative thinking about the best ways to design and implement the training program. But leaders from the two Colleges of Education and from Hotam had different views about what knowledge teachers need, who is the best teacher educator, how teachers can learn what they need to know, and so on. These differences created tensions and conflicts in the first year of the program.

Some tensions involved curriculum organization. Conventional teacher education programs divide the curriculum by discipline (educational sociology, psychology, etc.). The academic team suggested that the knowledge be organized around authentic issues arising from personal and contextual matters and concerns.

Another tension came from the desire of Hotam organization leaders to take charge of leadership and activism. The academic team viewed the development of these capacities as cross-cutting threads in the curriculum as a whole, rather than separate components.

Tensions also revolved around who should serve as teacher educators, what they should teach, and when. While the Hotam people thought in terms of clear boundaries between different courses and different types of teacher educators, the academic team suggested crossing disciplinary boundaries, relying on fewer teacher educators and planning fewer courses in order to achieve more coherence and focus on authentic issues and big ideas.

A major stumbling block was the nature of the content to be taught during the first year of training. The Hotam organization insisted that the focus be on practical tools to address the immediate needs of teachers. The academic leaders pointed out the limitation of such a focus. They recommended an emphasis on the ability to ask questions and act in an uncertain reality.

The following two stories illustrate some of these tensions and dilemmas. Ran, a new teacher, was required to prepare his students for the matriculation exam in mathematics only four months into the school year. His class consisted of under-privileged students, with very low levels of math and low motivation and self-esteem. As a new math teacher in a very complex socio-cultural context, Ran felt that he had to fulfill the expectations and lead his class to a high level of achievements.

The challenge he faced raised basic questions about learning, teaching, and evaluation. Ran asked himself whether the right way to teach is to supply the narrow knowledge needed to pass the tests or to teach in the way he was learning about in the training program which emphasized understanding and developing high levels of mathematical thinking. He asked himself: "What are my aims? Am I teaching for the short term or working to develop students' broad mathematical thinking so that they can explore different ways of learning and discover possible answers to complex mathematical problems?"

Ran chose the fast, narrow path, which would improve students' achievement in a short time and give them a chance to pass the test. For those four months, he provided his students with the basic knowledge required to pass the test. But, from this experience and from his deliberation about his role as a math teacher, he developed his own understanding, his personal stance, and a multidimensional approach responsive to different aspects of the teaching-learning process.

Another story that highlights the complexity we faced concerned the organization of the summer school where Hotam alumni serve as mentor teachers. Graduates of previous cohorts, these mentors brought an approach to learning and teaching based on a fixed notion of how a lesson should be planned and structured. They insisted on teaching the Hotamists set procedures and specific tools for each part of a lesson: what a teacher should say when entering the class, basic rules regarding pupils' behavior, specific stages for leading a lesson, and so on.

This approach contradicted the approach of the new program, which emphasized Hotamists' studying the needs of the real experience and drawing on their experiences. We encouraged students to ask questions about the specific needs of the pupils and the specific characteristics of the situation rather than giving them clear answers about what to do.

We found ourselves dealing with two different languages which created tensions and conflicts. The need to manage these differences generated ongoing debate and discussions through which we clarified and conceptualized basic assumptions and beliefs. In dealing with these differences, we learned to treat them as dilemmas to struggle with rather than problems to solve once and for all.

We realized that flexibility, openness, and confidence were required in order to agree on the optimal experiences for our students and identify the critical outcomes and deep learning processes that would challenge old and conventional assumptions and enable real change.

YEAR ONE: FROM VISION TO REALITY

Admission to the program was very competitive. We began with 114 participants, selected from among 2,700 applicants. The heterogeneous group consisted of Jews, Muslim, and Christian Arabs, men and women, Israeli-born and immigrants. Participants came from all parts of the country and had a variety of academic backgrounds.

The principles of the innovative training program guided the recruitment of staff members, the choice of training content, the structuring of the learning and mentoring environments, and curricular frameworks. These principles were translated into conceptual, organizational, and pedagogical aspects of the training.

Conceptual Thinking

The Hotam vision rests on the assumption that by providing children with an excellent education, Hotamists would be agents of change, making a difference in children's lives by transforming their futures. This vision guided the design of the training program.

Because most of the training takes place while Hotamists work almost full-time as teachers, most of the teaching and learning is based on their experiences in the field. They bring these experiences to their lessons, where they are analyzed and conceptualized through the lens of theory. Encountering multiple ways to understand the same issues helps Hotamists (re-)frame their understandings of classrooms and students, gain insights into their practice, and improve their teaching.

Being a teacher involves more than teaching particular subject(s). It requires viewing the class and the students as mirrors of social reality, shaping a vision, and creating a web of partners to realize that vision. Training in educational leadership involves developing the ability and commitment to define goals, come up with creative solutions to present challenges, and take actions that generate cooperation and enthusiasm with all the parties involved. In this way, Hotamists become activist agents of change.

The central belief undergirding the program is that Hotamists' experiences as learners affect their abilities as teachers. Consequently we sought teacher educators who could serve as models and sources of inspiration, professionals who would "walk the talk" and practice what they preached. The teacher educators had to be attuned to what they could learn from the Hotamists, engage the entire group, and adapt their goals to Hotamists' concern. They had to see themselves as guides for their students, reflecting on what was discussed each day and how to refocus students on their own goals.

The emergent curriculum was constructed around relevant issues, significant theory, and a common vision. The common vision focused on the following question: How can I take action and how can I change and improve in order to better facilitate students' advancement?

In order to develop leadership skills, Hotamists were expected to initiate action and develop their own ideas. Active learning became a dominant principle, operationalized though the different formats of the training program—self-chosen groups, learning days, fixed times for peer learning, round tables, invited conferences, and so on.

The pressing need to develop professional skills and knowledge in a short time under extreme school conditions highlighted the priority for learning to integrate different kinds of knowledge and skills. We aspired to construct an integrated, coherent curriculum, focused on a vision of teaching and learning, and shared understandings about how to organize learning opportunities.

Organizational Thinking

The year-long training program paralleled the school calendar rather than the academic calendar. Based on the process that new teachers go through during their first year of teaching, the program was divided into 6 stages: (1) pre-training (May–July); (2) pre-field experience (first two weeks in July); (3) summer school (last two weeks of July); (4) "jumping into the cold water" (beginning classroom teaching) (August–December); (5) adjustment (December–March); (6) looking toward the end and next steps. The content was adjusted to each stage and its unique requirements.

The entire training was divided between the five weeks of summer training under residential-school conditions and the year-long training during the school year. This took place once a week, nine hours a day, for thirty-one weeks.

During the summer training and after the first week in the program, Hotamists had an opportunity to teach pupils who attended a two-week summer school. Each Hotamist was required to teach six lessons, to be observed and get feedback from the program staff. These six lessons were the only field experience the Hotamists brought to the real work of teaching. They served as the starting point of their professional development as Hotamist teachers.

In order to help Hotamists overcome their fear of the unknown and provide access to people who could answer their questions, some staff were alumni of the Hotam program. These alumni had undergone a similar experience during the previous year and could provide support based on firsthand knowledge.

In order to realize the principle of integration, the training program was structured around modules rather than courses. The four modules were: (a) the socio-cultural context of the larger society, (b) the educational system and school system, (c) the Hotamist personal-professional context of forming identities as teacher leaders, and (d) the classroom teaching and learning practices.

The training mainly took place in two social structures. Home-based groups, defined by the geographical location of the schools where Hotamists taught, provided the context for discussing generic pedagogical subjects. Subject-matter groups provided the setting for dealing with subject-matter specific issues. Each group was led by professional staff that were responsible for training during the summer and during the school year.

During the schoolyear, the training day schedule followed a fixed schedule: 9:00 am–12:00 pm: study in the home-based groups; 1:00 pm–2:00 pm: peer and independent learning; 2:00 pm–5:00 pm: study in subject-matter groups. Special events took place with three frameworks developed by the staff: (a) *Zavta* (learning together), (b) self-guided regional tours, (c) *Mikudia* (focusing learning).

Zavata was based on teams of Hotamists planned a conference and led peer learning around issues based on their practice. *Regional tours*, planned and led by home groups, enabled the whole cohort to study educational challenges specific to each region. For example, the Jerusalem home group organized a tour emphasizing the challenges of a multicultural society in conflict in Jerusalem. *Mikudia* was based on small group meetings for the Hotamists around different issues planned by the staff, each staff member taking charge of three meetings in his/her area of expertise.

The main context for studying and developing students' self-perception and professional identity as educational leaders was the group. This reflects Hotam's goal of creating communities of educators in different geographical regions who can influence the schools and region in the years ahead. It is reinforced by theories about the formation of teachers' professional identity and theories of social change (Shadmi-Wortman, 2012).

In particular, we were influenced by the concept of the Bonding Community Team (BCT) (Shadmi-Wortman, 2012) which combines a common task and interpersonal relationships. As a community framework, the bonding community team emphasizes a common vision, shared living/mutual trust, and a joint mission. It serves as both means and end in the program.

Pedagogical Thinking

Ideally, staff members should have school experience as teachers or managers with under-privileged or at-risk learners or experience in teacher training. They need the ability to lead groups, work in teams, and learn and develop. They should also believe that education can change reality and be committed to social change for social justice. Meeting all these conditions was challenging, and our staff worked hard to learn, adjust to the uniqueness of the program, and complement each other.

Each home-based group was jointly led and taught by two staff members with different profiles: (a) an academic staff member, usually more experienced in fieldwork and teaching, and in social activism with broad professional theoretical perspectives, and (b) a Hotam staff member, sometimes a Hotam alumnus, usually younger than the academic staff with few years of experience in teaching.

Both leaders functioned with mutual responsibility. The academic staff member was in charge of the academic aspects; the Hotam staff member was in charge of supporting Hotamists in their fieldwork. Together they created the best conditions for a synergy between theory and practice.

The program emphasized the autonomy of the Hotamist as a learner. This was achieved by promoting leadership skills and conducting workshops based on the learner's self-responsibility, active learning, and involvement in decisions regarding what should be learned, how, and when teaching should take place.

The process of the training was based on high demands for learning and professionalism from staff and Hotamists. Both faced challenges that often involved frustrations. By handling these challenges together, the staff developed the Hotamists' ability to take risks, cope with ambiguity, exercise judgment, and act autonomously.

Teaching experience was the main platform for connecting practice and theory: When staff members introduced theoretical issues in their lessons, field experience provided evidence or illustration. When students brought case studies based on their experiences in classrooms, theoretical knowledge was used to interpret the case. Often lessons were videotaped for analysis in the training class.

Designing an Evaluation Process

One of the biggest challenges was developing an evaluation process consistent with the program's guiding principles. We adopted a framework called

"empowerment evaluation" (Fetterman, 2001, 2009) which uses evaluation concepts and techniques to foster improvement and self-determination. This approach involves community members in their own evaluation rather than placing the responsibility in the hands of external evaluators. It fit our emphasis on democratic participation, collaboration, commitment, and accountability.

Based on these principles, the staff developed an alternative assessment which provides an overall impression of each Hotamist's professional development throughout the program. This process has several components. At the end of each of the six stages in the school-year cycle, Hotamists write a reflective assignment about their professional development as learners and teachers grounded in evidence collected from practice. Hotamists analyze this evidence, using theoretical knowledge studied in their home-based and subject matter groups.

At the end of the training, each Hotamist presents his/her teaching-learning journey to the staff and colleagues, who provide feedback. At the final stage of training, the Hotamists and the staff fill out a form designed by the staff which refers to the Hotamists' personal and professional development. Besides their formal certificate, Hotamists receive a special certificate written by the staff members involved in their training. It contains detailed feedback about the Hotamist's personal and professional development. It also identifies developmental challenges for the future.

INSIGHTS FROM THE FIRST YEAR, LOOKING FORWARD TO THE SECOND YEAR

Results from an internal evaluation report conducted by the Hotam organization every year reveals high success regarding participants' satisfaction with innovative aspects of the programs. For instance, 89% of Hotamists indicated high to very high satisfaction with the training process and its relevance to their experience in school. Most regarded the groups as safe spaces and supportive settings. They also viewed the staff as a source of inspiration, encouraging them to clarify their beliefs and develop their ability to lead change.

The innovative teacher-education program offered all participants, staff, and Hotamists a new kind of experience, based on a new approach to learning, knowing, and learning by doing. The intense schedule set high expectations. Participants emphasized the benefits of being involved in their own learning. They also cited the continuity of the training and the stability of the staff, groups, and schedule as strong points of the program.

As with any innovative programs, many ad hoc decisions changes were made as the program unfolded. The first year challenged everyone, raising many questions about how to prepare for the next cohort. Given the environment and reality in which the program operates and given our values and beliefs, most of the fundamental dilemmas raised in the first year have persisted.

One issue concerned the discontinuity between the schools and the training program which prevented us from creating a holistic experience (Shani, 2010). We believe that closer partnerships between the schools where Hotamists teach and the Hotam Naomi training program can offer opportunities for ongoing professional development and promote mutual responsibility for the improvement of student achievement.

A second issue concerned the at-risk children and youth with whom the Hotamists work. We wonder whether this requires a special pedagogical approach or a different kind of training to address the unique characteristics of the school populations being served. We also puzzled about how to prepare Hotamists to be agents of change while also learning to function in the existing system.

As the first year ends and the second begins, we are dealing with these issues. We are adapting the emergent curriculum of the Hotam Naomi education program to our new insights and new circumstances. We are challenging what we have taken for granted and changing the program through authentic deliberation among all the partners.

THOUGHTS FOR THE FUTURE

All teacher educators face similar dilemmas and challenges in designing a new program. What is the place of academic experts and experts from the field? What should the relative emphasis be on pedagogical knowledge and self-understanding, immediate solutions and practical tools, broader perspectives and specific techniques? Should mentors give novices answers or should they teach them to ask questions and arrive at their own judgments? Is collaboration more important than autonomy? Are different areas of expertise more valuable than integration?

What distinguishes a program is the way it addresses these enduring dilemmas. These are not technical decisions. Rather they rest on the values and beliefs of program leaders about who are the best future teachers for our society and how they can best be prepared for their critical and challenging responsibilities. Moreover, they rest on an ongoing reflective process and a continuous dialogue between all the parties.

We defined the dilemmas and came up with answers, recognizing the costs and benefits of each decision. Loyalty to the program's vision became the main guideline and source of inspiration: *To raise the next generation of teachers who are social leaders devoted to social justice as the platform for a resilient society.* Hopefully the program takes a successful first step toward this vision.

REFERENCES

Fetterman, D. M. (2001). *Foundations of empowerment evaluation.* Thousand Oaks, CA: Sage.
Fetterman, D. M. (2009). Empowerment evaluation at the Stanford University School of Medicine: Using a critical friend to improve the clerkship experience. *Ensaio: Avaliação e Políticas Públicas em Educação, Rio de Janeiro, 17*(63), 197–204.
Grinfeld, N., & Barlev, B. (2013). Ha agaf lehachsharat ovdei horaha: Mediniut ve mahase [The department of teacher training: Policy and practice]. In S. Shimoni & O. Avidav-Unger (Eds.), *Al harezef: Hachshara, hitmahut vepituah mikzohi shel morim—Mediniut, teoria vemahase* [On the continuum: Training, specialization, and teachers' professional development—Policy, theory, and practice] (pp. 27–60). Tel Aviv: MOFET (Hebrew).
Ministry of Education & Council of Higher Education. (2006). *Mitvim manhim lehachshara lahoraha bemosdot lehaskala gvoha be Israel* [Ariav Report: Outlines of teacher education program in Israel]. http://cms.education.gov.il/EducationCMS/Units/HachsharatOvdey Horaa/Hozrim/MitveTudatHhoraa.htm (Hebrew).
Shadmi-Wortman, S. (2012). *Chevruta—Identity and its connection to social capital in the community (Pedagogy of identity in three arenas of action, 1989–2006)* (Unpublished doctoral dissertation). Tel Aviv University, Tel Aviv (Hebrew).
Shani, M. (2010). Likrat tfisa ecologit shel shiluv [Toward an ecological approach to inclusion]. In I. Margolin (Ed.), *Meever la Nahar: Netiv Hachshara Rav-masluli- Hachsharat morim kerav sihaj* [Crossing the beyond: A multi-track teacher education program—an ongoing discourse (pp. 148–170). Tel Aviv: MOFET & Levinsky College of Education (Hebrew).
Zeichner, K., & Pea-Sandoval, C. (2015). Venture philanthropy and teacher education policy in the U.S.: The role of the new schools venture fund. *Teachers College Record, 117*(6), 1–44.

Chapter Four

Employment-Based Teacher Education

A Partnership for Meeting the Needs of Underserved Learners in New Zealand

Ngaire Hoben

He aha te mea nui o te ao, He tāngata, he tāngata, he tāngata.
(What is the most important thing in the world? It is the people, it is the people, it is the people.)
—Māori whakatauki (proverb)

Since 2011 an employment-based pathway into teaching has developed from a partnership between a fledgling charitable trust and a faculty long-established in the field of initial teacher education. What brought TeachFirst NZ and the University of Auckland together was a shared concern for the absence of equity of outcome for a significant number of students in Aotearoa New Zealand (NZ) and a shared desire to do something to ensure that all learners have the opportunity to achieve their potential.

While NZ students enjoy high levels of success in international comparisons, NZ is categorized in reports from the Organization for Economic Cooperation and Development (OECD) as a "high achievement, low equity country" (Ministry of Education, 2015a). The gap between high and low performing students in Aotearoa NZ is one of the widest in the twenty-five countries within the OECD. Data from international tests such as the Program for International Student Assessment (PISA), and from national sources such as the National Certificate for Educational Achievement (NCEA) and national literacy and numeracy tests confirm the disparity in learning outcomes for particular groups of students within Aotearoa NZ. Māori and Pasifika students do not enjoy the same outcomes as other Pakeha (European) and Asian students (Ministry of Education, 2015a).

TeachFirst NZ proposed to address this inequity by recruiting successful graduates to work in schools serving lower socio-economic communities. The organization sought partnership with the Faculty of Education at the University of Auckland to develop and deliver an initial teacher education program with the express mission of reducing inequality.

This decision was not without controversy within the faculty and the wider education sector. Some critics opposed the "alliance" between the university and an organization with close links to the American organization, Teach For All. Others opposed what was perceived to be the neo-liberal agenda of that organization and the use of private sector or entrepreneur funding to support public schooling, which they believed should be adequately funded by the government. These were just two of the objections raised by those who opposed the initiative.

This chapter focuses on the nature of the program developed by the partnership. The program's success lies in its adherence to the vision of equity of outcome for all students regardless of ethnicity or school attended, and to the emphasis on professional relationships of care that permeate the program. "Care" incorporates a commitment to ensuring that teachers hold the highest of expectations that their students can and will succeed. Besides doing their very best to engage and motivate students to academic achievement, our teachers are explicitly establishing the foundations for life as a learner beyond school.

Why This Program Is Needed

Committed to addressing educational disparity, TeachFirst NZ and the University of Auckland formed a partnership to design a new pathway into teaching. From the university's point of view, novice teachers graduating from the traditional, mainstream secondary initial teacher education (ITE) program were not electing to enter schools serving lower socio-economic communities. Consequently, schools serving lower socio-economic communities struggle to recruit qualified teachers, particularly in so-called hard-to-staff subjects of physics, maths, chemistry, Te reo Māori, and English.

TeachFirst NZ's commitment to addressing disparity is reflected in its vision statement: *That all young people in Aotearoa New Zealand achieve their full potential.* In addition, TeachFirst NZ is committed to developing people who will go on to become leaders in either education or the world beyond. Their alumni are charged with the task of continuing to work for equity of educational outcome whether they remain in the classroom or seek other occupations.

Secondary schools in Aotearoa NZ serve students in grades nine through thirteen, who tend to be between thirteen and eighteen years old. TeachFirst NZ seeks positions for its participants in secondary schools in Auckland and

Northland, in hard-to-staff schools with high proportions of Māori and Pasifika students. In Auckland, these tend to be located in low socio-economic communities on the fringes of the city. Northland, an area north of Auckland, has a high Māori population and the highest unemployment in Aotearoa NZ. The distance from Auckland makes it difficult for the faculty to visit participants, who must travel considerable distance to clinics. But such placements enable participants with families to do the program and remain in their home communities.

Meeting the Needs of Underserved Students

Animated by our vision to serve underserved students, the TeachFirst NZ program has the following features:

- Rigorous selection
- A summer intensive, providing preparation prior to starting teaching
- The opportunity to establish a community of practice
- A manageable teaching load for new teachers
- "Just in time" provision of teaching and learning strategies
- A coherent integration of theory and practice.
- In-school mentoring
- Regular school visits by a small team of curriculum specialists
- Fostering the development of a culturally relevant pedagogy of relations.

Each of these features is elaborated below to assist readers in gaining a clear understanding of how the program works.

Rigorous selection. Selection into the program is managed by TeachFirst NZ, which operates an energetic, sophisticated, and thorough recruitment and selection process. Applicants apply online. Those who meet eligibility requirements are invited to a full-day assessment. Applicants have two individual interviews, participate in a group task, teach a sample lesson, and reflect on their performance at various points in the day. In keeping with the goal of attracting highly qualified graduates into teaching, a grade point average (GPA) of B+ is required for all participants.

The size of the cohort is dictated by the funding, which the Ministry of Education initially committed to a four-year pilot and has recently extended for two additional years, and by the Education Council of Aotearoa NZ, which approved a cohort of twenty participants qualified to teach in the hard-to-staff subjects of math, physics, chemistry, Te reo Māori, and English. Aspiring teachers must have an undergraduate degree with advanced study (i.e., a major) in a subject taught between the ages nine and thirteen in a secondary school, which further constrains the potential pool of applicants.[1]

Approximately 6 percent of those making an initial application finally secure a place in the program. The recruitment and selection team manages to maintain selection criteria, while simultaneously striving for a demographic balance in those selected. The fact that university fees are paid and participants receive an untrained teacher's salary over the two years of teaching and concurrent study are attractive features of the program, given that no other ITE program provides study fees or payment.

There has been a concerted effort to attract Māori, Pasifika, and male students into the program and to increase numbers in the STEM subjects of math, physics, and chemistry. The way in which the academic program is delivered, via a seven-week summer intensive and well-spaced clinics, combined with the payment of a salary and the possibility of teaching close to one's home, has enabled four highly qualified, mature women with families to undertake the program from their homes in the far north of Aotearoa NZ, an area which struggles even more than the urban location of Auckland to recruit qualified teachers in hard-to-staff subjects.

The Council-imposed constraint on recruiting only twenty participants has two advantages: it is easier to establish a close-knit community of practice and to keep a close eye on the balance of the cohort. If a choice must be made among equally well-qualified applicants, men enjoy a greater chance of selection than women, as the imbalance of men to women in the teaching profession in NZ has become a source of considerable concern.

The summer intensive. The program begins with a very full seven-week residential "intensive." Participants attend campus-based courses from 8:15 am to 5:30 pm, visit schools, and teach in a week-long summer teaching period when school-aged students come into the university to work on developing skills before the school year begins. By the end of the summer, participants have completed one quarter of the academic credits required for their Post-Graduate Diploma in Teaching (Secondary Field-Based), the academic qualification attached to the program.

The opportunity to establish a community of practice. Key to the summer intensive's success and to the program overall is the building of a sense of whānau[2] (family) among the participants. The first event is a noho marae. The cohort lives together for two days on the university marae and begins to develop an understanding of tikanga Māori and of the concepts of manaakitanga and whanaungatanga.

For many this is their first experience of Māori culture up close. Although discomforting, virtually all concede that it is a high point in their summer intensive, opening their eyes, hearts, and minds to the culture and values of New Zealand's indigenous population in new ways. The experience of living together in a university hall of residence over this seven-week period establishes a very strong bond among the cohort.

Conditions of employment. Participants' school employment begins at the end of January, the start of the school year in Aotearoa NZ. Participants teach a reduced load of three classes, considered manageable for a novice teacher undertaking concurrent study. These as-yet unqualified teachers work as teachers of record under the auspices of a Limited Authority to Teach (LAT), granted by the Education Council of Aotearoa New Zealand.

The academic program continues for two years while participants teach in schools serving a lower decile community. Academic classes are held on five occasions during the year, at four clinics and a brief mid-year residential. The clinics begin on Friday afternoon and continue through Saturday, with participants meeting in small groups for curriculum-focused sessions and as a cohort for instruction on more generic aspects of teaching and learning.

Topics meet participants' developing understanding and skill. For example, topics early in year one might include managing group work effectively, developing a more nuanced understanding of cultural responsiveness, and learning to implement the principles of differentiation. John Hattie's focus on effective teaching strategies is a shared text to stimulate discussion about classroom practices that impact student learning (Hattie, 2012).

Teaching as inquiry (Ministry of Education, 2007, 35) is promoted and modeled from the outset. During their first year, participants study the impact of their teaching on three students as part of their academic course work.[3] Between the first and second years of teaching, participants take an academic credit course on practitioner research. Then in year two, they investigate an aspect of their own practice.

A coherent integration of theory and practice. The focus on *teaching as inquiry*[4] supports participants in understanding and connecting theory and practice. During the summer intensive, participants are challenged to make sense of the theory being taught. Moving into their classrooms at the end of summer intensive enables participants to connect theory and practice in an authentic setting. These connections are reinforced during the clinic sessions when participants are better positioned to understand how theory can be enacted in the classroom.

In-school mentoring. One unusual feature of this program is the provision of a time allowance for mentors. The Ministry of Education provides funds to release mentors from one-fifth of their teaching programs to undertake this work. The quality of mentoring is crucial to participants' development as teachers (Humphrey & Wechsler, 2005).

The university provides three days of mentor training for teachers selected as mentors. This training promotes educative mentoring (Feiman-Nemser, 2001a, 2001b), which encourages an inquiry stance toward teaching and learning (Earl & Timperley, 2009). In addition, mentors attend a brief meeting after school once a term.

Regular visits by a small team of curriculum specialists. This field-based program represents a departure for the Education Council which approves all ITE programs. One condition of program approval was that participants would be visited fifteen times in their first year and up to ten times in their second year by university-appointed curriculum specialists. (Typically, pre-service teachers enrolled in one-year "mainstream," campus-based program are visited three times, while undertaking supervised teaching practice [practicum] in the classroom of a registered teacher.) The difference in requirements reflects the Council's caution in approving an alternative program and the fact that these new untrained teachers are teachers of record.

The University has appointed a small team of curriculum specialists to undertake these visits. The team meets regularly for their own professional development and to ensure consistent guidance. Visits typically include an observation followed by a conversation focused on the practice observed. Professional learning sessions for the visiting team emphasize the need to focus on the ways in which the lesson contributes to the learning of the pupils.

Fostering the development of a culturally relevant pedagogy of relations. Since the twenty participants in this partnership program are all teaching in schools with a high proportion of Māori and/or Pasifika students, every effort is made to help them learn to enact a culturally responsive pedagogy of relations. As Bishop (2010) states:

> A pedagogy of relations . . . means that learners can bring who they are to the classroom in complete safety. The fact that their knowledges are acceptable is central to this exercise. . . . Such a classroom will generate totally different interaction patterns and educational outcomes from a classroom where knowledge is seen as something that the teacher makes sense of and then passes onto students and will be conducted within and through a pedagogy of relations, wherein self-determining individuals interact with one another within non-dominating relations of interdependence. (Bishop, 2010, 167–169)

Guiding Ideas

The three principles that inform the program's design:

1. All students are capable of effective learning. Students are culturally located individuals. In Aotearoa New Zealand, the aim of education is to maximize the potential of every student.
2. Highly effective teachers can improve the academic and social outcomes for all students, and contribute significantly to a reduction in educational disparity by having high expectations of their students, and developing for each of them aspirational goals and a sense of possibility in their life choices.

3. To produce highly effective, inspirational teachers in Aotearoa New Zealand, initial teacher education (ITE) must be responsive to, and use current international and national research, (especially related to effective pedagogy), government/national educational policies (especially those related to curriculum and assessment and qualifications), and Ministry of Education strategies (especially those addressing disparity). ITE must develop knowledge of and integrate both theory and good practice over time; draw on the expertise of both teacher educators and school-based mentors; and offer multiple pathways into teaching (University of Auckland, 2011).

The theory of teaching underpinning this program rests on a view of the effective teacher as an adaptive expert (Bransford, Derry, Berliner, & Hammerness, with Beckett, 2005). Such a teacher has knowledge of learners and how they learn, knowledge of a subject and how to teach it, understanding of assessment and how best to use it to promote learning, and above all, knowledge of how to create a safe and inclusive learning environment in which all this can happen.

The adaptive expert teacher has deep subject and pedagogical content knowledge, knows when to question assumptions, and how to study the impact of his or her practice and identify the gaps in his or her own learning (Bransford et al., 2005; Timperley, 2013). Participants in TeachFirst NZ are constantly challenged to examine their practice, seek guidance, and deepen their understanding when confronted with a problem of practice.

Twice a year, participants lead a triadic discussion with the school-based mentor and visiting curriculum specialist. The discussion is framed around the identification of a problem or challenge which the participant is facing. Participants must gather video evidence of their initial practice and of their practice modified after they have investigated what the research literature has to say about the matter. The mentor and visiting specialist engage in a discussion with the participant, offering suggestions for further changes.

Is This an "Alternative" ITE Program?

The field-based program outlined above is definitely an "alternative" to traditional pathways into secondary teaching in Aotearoa NZ. While the term "field-based" is used in the title of the credential, a more accurate descriptor is "employment-based." In that respect, the program is an alternative to the regular or traditional pre-service program which offers sixteen weeks of academic coursework on campus and 14 weeks of school-based practicum in classrooms of fully licensed teachers who act as mentors, providing opportunities for supervised teaching practice.

The program is also an "alternative" to traditional pathways to teaching in that the sites for practice are restricted to schools serving lower socio-economic communities. Participants make a two-year commitment to work in these schools as the teacher of record for each of those two years.

Some insist on referring to the program as a "fast-track" pathway into teaching. In reality, it takes two years and two months for TeachFirst NZ participants to become provisionally registered teachers, a status that traditional pathway pre-service teachers in traditional programs reach in thirty weeks.

Strengths and Limitations of This Model

The greatest strength of the program is the shared commitment of all concerned to the mission of the program—to address educational inequality. This involves a close working partnership with a number of very special schools and their teachers and students. With the support of a trained and positive mentor, novice teachers with strong academic credentials and a strong sense of personal agency can begin their teaching careers with a manageable teaching load and develop their practice under the watchful and skilled tutelage of mentors and visiting teachers.

A second strength is the emergence of a cohesive community of practitioners, with a strong sense of whanaungatanga. Participants constitute a community of learners focused on a shared mission and available as a group to engage in discussions about teaching and learning, and take action regarding the challenges faced by students and their schools in Aotearoa NZ at this time.

A third strength for those who work in the program is the satisfaction of delivering a program developed around a shared vision and underpinned by a theory of effective teaching which shapes the program's content as well as the way in which classroom teaching is assessed for both formative and summative purposes.

Limitations exist as well. For TeachFirst NZ, these include the constraints placed on the size of each intake (twenty participants) and the subject range. For the university, a major limitation is the cost. There is no economy of scale in teaching such small numbers and the costs of visiting participants in their classrooms on the scale required by the Education Council of Aotearoa New Zealand are great.

The University is also concerned about the adequacy of the preparation participants receive in advance of assuming responsibility for three classes. Because the summer intensive occurs during the school vacation, participants cannot have an extended experience in "real" schools. At this stage in their preparation, they have limited understanding of classroom practice and much of what is taught in summer intensive can seem very abstract.

Most participants begin teaching on a near vertical learning curve. In those first weeks, they are processing an enormous amount of new information with very little understanding of how schools operate. It takes many of them several months to fully grasp how a teaching program relates to the curriculum and how to plan to meet the needs of their students.

This is probably of greater concern to initial teacher educators than to others. Principals are realistic about the amount of support all beginning teachers require and do not find TeachFirst NZ participants less prepared than any other beginning teacher. The participants themselves reflect both ends of the "confidence" spectrum. One participant told the New Zealand Council for Educational Research (NZCER) evaluators:

> It was a smooth transition into becoming a teacher—we were well prepared with teaching strategies and understanding psychology of the brain, and why students behave the way they do, but needed a little more on subject content and teaching NCEA (the national qualification). (Ministry of Education, 2015b, 19)

A second participant was more fatalistic about the impossibility of *ever* being adequately prepared for a job like teaching:

> I don't think it's possible to prepare. You just need to understand [that] when you get here you will flounder. That's just the nature of the beast. (Ministry of Education, 2015b, 19)

The professional community sees this pathway as a threat to the profession because it challenges the status quo and turns upside down the way the way things have been for the past eight decades. Some assert that the real beneficiaries of programs like TeachFirst NZ are the participants themselves, not their students. Our experience is that pupils benefit as well. The results achieved in the National Certificate of Educational Achievement by the students of a significant number of the participants demonstrate this, although no empirical study has been undertaken to date.

Is the Program Achieving What It Set Out to Achieve?

Impact on pupil learning is naturally of concern to all involved. TeachFirst NZ is answerable to their financial backers and the global network of Teach For All, both of which are more focused on *immediate* impact than the university. The university certainly wants this pathway to help achieve equity of outcome. It recognizes, however, that such an impact is larger than what one novice teacher can achieve in a single year. Rather, it is the cumulative effect of a focus on *teaching as inquiry*, reflection, and educative mentoring that will ultimately affect the achievement of the students of these novice teachers.

The program has been extensively evaluated since its inception. NZCER has conducted an annual evaluation for the four years of the pilot and their reports to the Ministry of Education for years one and two have been publicly released. The most recent concluded:

> Teach First NZ programme is being implemented effectively and efficiently, and has benefited rather than suffered from doubling in size.[5] Improvements have been made to the programme in 2014, based on feedback from 2013. The Teach First NZ partnership continues to find ways to strengthen the pro-gramme and to ensure it is well known and well supported. Participants are very strong ambassadors for the programme and for secondary teaching in New Zealand. Almost all participants have achieved highly, have supported their students to do well, including in NCEA, and intend to stay in teaching at least in the short term. (Ministry of Education, 2015b, 52)

Stakeholders are well positioned to comment on the strength of the program. A group of principals who have employed these teachers speak positively about the experience:

> We can confirm that TeachFirst NZ participants are held in high regard by the staff and principals of the schools in which they serve . . . they have an excellent command of their specialist subjects and because they are also care-fully selected for their attitude and dispositions, their relationships with stu-dents are positive, energetic and respectful.

> By applying for the program, TeachFirst NZ participants choose to contribute to enhancing the potential of students who are often disadvantaged, but they also understand that they are privileged to work in these communities and to learn from their students and their families and whānau. Individually they make a significant contribution in the classroom, in the co-curriculum and by participating in the wider school community. (Letter from the Counties Manu-kau Principals, November 4, 2014)

NOTES

1. In the Uniteed Kingdom, for example, TeachFirst applicants are required to have an A level pass in a subject they wish to teach. Entry requirements in New Zealand constrain the numbers eligible for selection.

2. These terms can be understood as follows: Whānau—extended family (Bishop, 2008) Noho marae—a learning experience gained by living on a marae Marae—courtyard, the open area in front of the wharenui, where formal greetings and discussions take place. Often also used to include the complex of buildings around the marae (http://maoridictionary.co.nz) (Bish-op 2008).

Tikanga Māori—the customary system of values and practices that have developed over time and are deeply embedded in the social context (http://maoridictionary.co.nz)

Manaakitanga—caring for students as culturally located human beings (Bishop, 2008)

Whanaungatanga—relationships with high expectations (Bishop, 2008)

3. Teaching as inquiry requires teachers to investigate the impact of their teaching practice on their students. It is described in *The New Zealand Curriculum* (Ministry of Education, 2007, 35) as a cyclical process in which teachers identify the learning needs of their students and plan their teaching programs to meet these needs. A stage in the cycle requires the teacher to examine the impact of their teaching on the learning outcomes for their students.

4. See *The New Zealand Curriculum*, elaborated on by Aitken & Sinnema (2008) and Timperley (2013).

5. As the program moved from the first to second year, the numbers doubled as the program is a two-year commitment, both in teaching and in studying.

REFERENCES

Aitken, G., & Sinnema, C. (2008) *Effective Pedagogy in the Social Sciences/tikanga ā iwi: Best evidence synthesis iteration (BES)*. Wellington, NZ: Ministry of Education.

Bishop, R. (2010). Diversity and educational disparities: The role of teacher education. In *Educating teachers for diversity: Meeting the challenge*. Paris: OECD Publishing.

Bransford, J., Derry, S., Berliner, D., & Hammerness, K., with Beckett, K. L. (2005). *Theories of Learning and Their Role in Teaching*. In L. Darling-Hammond & J. Bransford (Eds.), *Preparing teachers for a changing world: What teachers should learn and be able to do*. San Francisco: Jossey-Bass.

Earl, L., & Timperley, H. (2009). Understanding how evidence and learning conversations work. In L. Earl & H. Timperley (Eds.), *Professional learning conversations: Challenges in using evidence for improvement* (pp. 1–12). Dordrecht, the Netherlands: Springer.

Feiman-Nemser, S. (2001a). From preparation to practice: Designing a continuum to strengthen and sustain teaching. *Teachers College Record, 103*(6), 1013–1051.

Feiman-Nemser, S. (2001b). Helping novices learn to teach: Lessons from an exemplary support teacher. *Journal of Teacher Education, 52*(1), 17–30.

Hattie, J. (2012). *Visible learning for teachers*. London: Routledge.

Humphrey, D. C., & Wechsler, M. E. (2005). Insights into alternative certification: Initial findings from a national study. *Teachers College Record, 109*(3), 483–530.

Ministry of Education. (2007). *The New Zealand Curriculum*. Wellington, New Zealand: Learning Media.

Ministry of Education. (2015a). PISA (Programme for International Student Assessement) 2012. Retrieved from http://www.educationcounts.govt.nz/publications/series/PISA/pisa-2012 and https://www.educationcounts.govt.nz/__data/assets/pdf_file/0004/144859/1015_PISA-Topline-Results.pdf.

Ministry of Education. (2015b). *2014 annual evaluation report for the TeachFirst NZ programme pilot delivered in partnership with the University of Auckland*. Wellington, New Zealand: NZCER.

Timperley, H. (2013). *Learning to practise in initial teacher education*. A paper for discussion. Wellington, NZ: Ministry of Education.

University of Auckland. (2011). Documentation to Teachers Council [now education Council of Aotearoa New Zealand] seeking approval for this program.

Chapter Five

Recruiting High-Performing Candidates to the Teaching Profession

Realities and Misconceptions

Zipora Libman

The past twenty years could be cast as a grand experiment to improve teacher quality through teacher labor market innovations. More employment opportunities for women, along with increased teacher retirements and rising demands on schools to serve broader populations of students have led policy makers worldwide to open new pathways to teaching. These interventions aim to increase the quality and supply of teachers (Henry, Bastian, & Smith, 2012).

In Israel, five special routes have been designed to attract high-performing candidates to the teaching profession. These innovations reflect the belief that increasing the human capital of the educator workforce would benefit both students and the teaching profession. Still, little evidence confirms the success of these interventions (Henry et al., 2012; Libman, Ackerman-Asher, & Maskit, 2013).

One such program, the Israeli Excellent Students Project (IESP), has garnered much attention. This prestigious, highly visible project recruits candidates with top SAT test scores and prepares them to become teachers through an accelerated, flexible program. For the past fifteen years, substantial sums of money have been invested in implementing the program, but little in evaluating it. This chapter reports on an evaluation study of IESP graduates, draws policy implications, and discusses ways to improve competitive scholarship programs as a lever for recruiting academically talented teachers.

Background

The recruitment and retention of academically talented teachers for public schools is a big challenge in education today, and there have been many attempts to attract high ability candidates to teaching. Countries like Sweden, France, Korea, and New Zealand have tried to make teaching more attractive to excellent candidates by experimenting with alternative routes, scholarships and incentives for professional development (European Union, 2013; OECD, 2011). Other innovative recruitment strategies, such as providing college scholarships to strong applicants who earn traditional teacher-preparation degrees and teach in public schools, exist in many places. Still, we know little about the effectiveness of such efforts.

The Israeli Context

Over the last twenty years, Israel's Ministry of Education has initiated five different scholarship programs for prospective teachers. The IESP aims to attract talented high school graduates into the teaching profession and help them develop leadership qualities, such as visionary thinking and activism. The program targets candidates with an SAT score that is at least two standard deviations above the required threshold score. Since the program's inception, Israel has funded annual cohorts of 300 candidates, providing them with full scholarship to attend a college of education and earn their academic requirements and teaching credential.

Academically able high school graduates are recruited through a rigorous multi-step process. Once accepted to the program, IESP candidates receive the same teacher education curriculum as other teacher candidates; however, they can meet the requirements in three rather than four years. They also participate in special enrichment activities such as seminars to discuss pedagogy and reflect on their development, cultural events and tours, service opportunities, and extensive tutoring and field experience. These activities are designed to encourage the development of leaders, provide a greater understanding of education's place in society and instill a sense of mission, service and professionalism.

IESP candidates are expected to "pay back" their scholarship by teaching in public schools one year for each year they received a scholarship. Approximately 7% of all candidates enrolled annually in teacher education programs in Israel have participated in this project.

The Study

The IESP evaluation described in this chapter focused on participants six to eight years after graduation.[1] It sought answers to the following questions: (1) What is their integration into teaching like? (2) What reasons do those who drop out give for leaving teaching? and (3) What factors predict job satisfaction for academically talented teachers?

Graduates from three IESP cohorts (2003, 2004, 2005) were sampled using a random-systematic sampling procedure. A control group was drawn from the Ministry of Education database. Approximately 50% of those sampled responded to the questionnaire for a total of 163 IESP and 305 non-IESP graduates.

The questionnaire, which included both closed and open items, was administered as a telephone survey. One section explored teachers' integration into the teaching profession. Sample questions included the following: Do you work as a teacher? For how many years? Where do you teach? If you aren't teaching, why not? How would you evaluate your teacher preparation program? Did you participate in an induction program? Would you choose teaching again as a career if you had it to do over? Are you satisfied as a teacher?

As Table 5.1 shows, the sample of respondents reflects three important indicators: year of graduation, religion, and grade level where the teachers work. It shows that there is no selection bias in the survey results.

Table 5.1.   The Sample

	IESP		Non-IESP	
	Total sample $n = 318$	Respondents' sample $n = 163$	Total sample $n = 759$	Respondents' sample $n = 305$
Year of graduation				
2003	28.6	29.4	27.7	29.8
2004	33.3	33.7	28.8	26.9
2005	38.1	36.9	43.5	43.4
	100.0	100.0	100.0	100.0
Sector				
Jewish	84.0	82.2	85.0	87.9
Arab	16.0	17.8	15.0	12.1
	100.0	100.0	100.0	100.0
Grade level				
Kindergarten	12.0	10.1	19.1	20.9
Elementary school	26.2	28.3	34.9	36.9
Middle school	18.1	16.2	10.7	8.2
High school	29.3	31.3	23.3	24.5
Other	14.4	13.1	9.9	5.5
	100.0	100.0	100.0	100.0

Data were analyzed using both quantitative and qualitative methods. Findings about respondents' integration into the teaching profession are presented below. They are based on descriptive and multivariate statistics and a content analysis of answers to the open-ended questions.

Integration into the Teaching Profession

To examine whether IESP graduates remained in teaching beyond the period required to fulfill the obligations of their scholarship, researchers tracked the three cohorts to see whether they persisted for six to eight years of teaching compared to the control group. The analysis considered three aspects of integration: (a) teachers' overall attrition rate; (b) differences in attrition rates between Jewish and Arab teachers, and (c) the size and scope of engagement in public vs. private schools.

Table 5.2 describes the percent of IESP graduates and control group graduates who were teaching six to eight years after graduation. Sixty percent of IESP graduates were working as teachers and there were no differences between IESP graduates and the control group regarding the proportion of graduates who were teaching.

Table 5.2.   Integration into the Teaching Profession (*n* = 468)

	IESP *n* = 163	Non-IESP *n* = 305	Total *n* = 468
Teachers *n* = 283	60.3	60.7	60.5
Non-teachers *n* = 185	39.7	39.3	39.5
	100.0	100.0	100.0

Attrition rates between Jewish and Arab teachers (see Table 5.3) show statistically significant differences (chi-square = 9.3; df = 1; $p < .005$). The attrition rate of graduates in the Jewish sector is higher compared to the Arab sector. In the Jewish sector, about 40% of all graduates, IESP and regular graduates, left teaching, while in the Arab sector, the percentage of non-teachers is smaller (about 25%). However, most of the Arab teachers who left teaching are IESP graduates; about 30% of Arab IESP graduates dropped out of teaching compared to 18% in the Arab control group. This unexpected finding may reflect limited employment options for educated Arabs in Israel. Also, excellent graduates may have many employment opportunities other than teaching.[2]

Table 5.3.   Integration into Teaching: Comparing Jewish and Arab Sector (n = 468)

	Jewish sector n = 412		Arab sector n = 56		Total n = 468	
	IESP	Control	IESP	Control	IESP	Control
Teachers n = 283	60.0	56.9	69.2	81.6	60.7	60.3
Non-teachers n = 185	40.0	43.1	30.8	18.4	39.3	39.7
	100.0	100.0	100.0	100.0	100.0	100.0

The survey also asked where teachers were teaching six to eight years after their graduation. This question is particularly important because IESP recipients are required to teach in public schools. Table 5.4 describes the percentages of teachers working in public schools as compared to the private sector at least two years after they fulfilled their formal requirement to teach in public schools.

Table 5.4.   Integration into Public vs. Private Sector (n = 283)

	IESP n = 99	Control n = 184	Total n = 283
Public schools	62.4	79.1	72.6
Private sector	37.6	20.9	27.4
	100.0	100.0	100.0

The percentage of IESP graduates who actually taught in the public system rather than in the private sector is smaller than in the control group (62% vs. 79% respectively, of the 60% who remained teachers). This difference was statistically significant (chi-square = 7.9; df = 1; $p < .005$), which raises a concern about the program since IESP graduates are required to pay back their scholarship by teaching in *public* schools. IESP teachers seem to have less of a commitment to teaching in public schools. At the same time, the public system does little to retain excellent teachers, many of whom move to the private sector (Libman et al., 2013).

Why do teachers drop out? Do IESP graduates give different reasons compared with their peers? Answers to these questions come from a content analysis of open-ended questions. Table 5.5 shows that IESP graduates have different reasons compared to the control group and these differences were statistically significant (chi-square = 16.08; df = 4; $p < .005$).

Table 5.5.   Teachers' Reasons for Dropping Out

	IESP $n = 64$	Control $n = 116$	Total $n = 180$
Working conditions	52.1	29.0	37.0
Didn't fit in	24.9	27.1	26.0
Didn't find a job	10.2	9.8	10.1
Personal, family reasons	7.8	11.8	10.9
Didn't intend to become teachers	5.0	22.2	16.0
	100.0	100.0	100.0

Many more IESP teachers who dropped out of teaching (almost 52%) were dissatisfied with extrinsic factors such as salary, working conditions, and school bureaucracy. By contrast, only 29% of the teachers in the control group identified those factors as reasons for their attrition. Here is how two teachers in the sample responded to the question of why they left teaching.

> All my life I wanted to become a teacher. I was an excellent student and had a wonderful experience as a member of IESP. But when I started working as a teacher, I realized how much effort and mental strength I have to invest in teaching every day from dawn till midnight. When everyday another "reform" falls on my head, I quickly understood that I must find myself a life and look for another profession.

> To tell you the truth, the salary was insulting; however, what depressed me most of all was the work conditions and lack of autonomy and trust. I felt I was not leading anything while everybody was telling me what to do, what to think and when to do what. As a professional who invested so much in becoming a teacher . . . I felt I was becoming smaller and smaller every day. It literally hurt my feelings.

Many IESP graduates had sincere, idealistic intentions to become teachers. While 22% of the "regular" graduates admitted that they never chose teaching as a permanent career and did not really intend to become teachers, only 5% of IESP graduates gave that answer. Yet almost a quarter of all teachers (IESP and non-IESP) decided not to become teachers because they felt that being a teacher required qualifications they did not have.

Given the care that goes into recruiting teachers for the IESP program, it is problematic that some graduates feel unprepared for teaching. What does this imply about the program? Equally problematic is the fact that almost 10% of the teachers dropped out for personal and family reasons and another 10% because they did not find jobs. (There were no significant differences between IESP and non-IESP candidates in that respect.) The fact that 10% of these promising graduates could not find teaching positions raises questions about what the program is doing to help graduate secure employment.

Teachers were asked the following question about job satisfaction: *On a 1 to 10 scale (10 being the highest), to what degree are you satisfied nowadays with the teaching profession?* They were also asked to explain in their own words what makes them satisfied and what disturbs them in their work.

Table 5.6.   Teachers' Job Satisfaction

Job satisfaction score	Frequency distribution (%) n = 283
<4	5.1
5 – 6	16.7
7 – 8	50.4
9 – 10	27.8
	100.0

Mean = 7.52, SD = 1.81.

As seen in Table 5.6, the teachers who persist in teaching are, to a certain extent, satisfied with their work as teachers. The mean job satisfaction score did not differ for IESP and non-IESP teachers (x = 7.52; s.d. = 1.81). In analyzing the factors that contribute to teachers' satisfaction or dissatisfaction with teaching, the researchers classified responses as individual, organizational, or transactional factors, then used a multiple regression analysis to evaluate the sources of graduates' job satisfaction.

The individual predictors were participation in IESP, religion, years of experience, and educational background. The organizational predictors were teacher preparation, teacher grade-level, school culture, and teacher participation in school decision-making. The transactional predictors were the effectiveness of induction, self-efficacy, and career satisfaction. The criterion variable was teachers' overall job satisfaction. Table 5.7 summarizes the results.

Table 5.7.   Predictors of Job Satisfaction

	b(SEb)	B	t
Individual factors			
IESP (yes/no)	.299(.276)	.084	1.082
Religion	-.020(.371)	-.004	-.054
Years of experience	-.002(.045)	-0.04	-.049
Educational background	-0.077(.143)	-.042	-.537
Organizational factors			
Teacher preparation	.015(.059)	.019	.247
Teacher grade level	.027(.081)	.026	.338

School culture/quality	.803(.177)	.334	4.548**
Teacher participation in school decision-making	.113(.264)	.032	.428
Transactional factors			
Effectiveness of induction	.162(.065)	.204	2.502*
Teacher self-efficacy	.120(.151)	.059	.792
Career satisfaction	.562(.411)	.100	1.363
Constant (a)	6.845(1.891)		
R^2	0.27		
F	3.913**		

* $p < .005$
** $p < .001$

The combination of all the predictors was significantly related to job satisfaction ($F = 3.913$; $p < .005$). The sample R square coefficient was .27, indicating that approximately 27% of variance of the job satisfaction index can be accounted for by the predictors. Studying Table 5.7, one sees that none of the individual factors, not even participation in IESP, was significant in predicting job satisfaction. The best predictor was an organizational factor: perceived school quality and culture ($\beta = .334$). The second significant predictor was a transactional factor: effectiveness of induction ($\beta = .204$). Career satisfaction was insignificant in explaining teachers' job satisfaction. This finding suggests that even the teachers who are dissatisfied with their current teaching situation do not regret choosing the teaching profession as their career.

Discussion

This study focused on a national effort to recruit and retain highly qualified candidates to the teaching profession in Israel. Like other research which seeks to determine teacher quality and its impact, this study was limited by the lack of validated measures of teacher quality and had to rely on indirect proxies such as teachers' background and scores on standardized tests, neither of which sheds light on candidates' teaching ability.

> Education advocates and policymakers have long argued that more academically able candidates should be recruited into teaching. But recruitment efforts are not enough. We must also retain these teachers in the system (Ingersoll, 2001). Successful retention of strong teachers would not only help raise the status of teaching, it would also increase a school's capacity for reform (European Union, 2013).

Past research on the impact of the IESP program suggests several reasons why IESP candidates may be more effective than other teachers (Libman,

2014). First, the program selects individuals with high levels of academic achievement which often correlate positively with student achievement gains (Clotfelter, Ladd, & Vigdor, 2010; Henry et al., 2012). Second, the IESP offers more extensive fieldwork opportunities and many multicultural and diversity experiences, which as recent research suggests, lead to more effective early career teaching (Boyd, Grossman, Lankford, Loeb, & Wyckoff, 2009). Finally, the IESP encourages the development of leadership and entrepreneurship and instills a strong sense of mission. This element distinguishes IESP from traditional preparation programs and may enhance its effectiveness.

The study found that the high-quality candidates who participated in this prestigious, scholarship-based program remained in teaching at exactly the same rates as other teachers. In both the IESP and the comparison group, 60% remained in teaching for six to eight years or more, while 40% dropped-out. These results challenge other studies which found that teachers with strong academic qualifications tend to leave the profession at higher rates than teachers with weaker qualifications (Borman & Dowling, 2008; Henry et al., 2012; Lankford, Loeb, McEachin, Miller, & Wyckoff, 2014).

Research on other programs designed to attract high-achieving candidates found mixed results. Most Teach For America corps members exit the profession after two or three years of teaching (Xu, Hannaway, & Taylor, 2011), whereas graduates of the North Carolina Teaching Fellows program stay in teaching longer than traditionally prepared teachers (Henry et al., 2012). The present survey indicates that IESP graduates' attrition rate is similar to other teachers.

Teacher retention is perceived as a measure of IESP effectiveness (e.g., Borman & Dowling, 2008). Still, assessing the impact of rigorous eligibility requirements and generous scholarships requires research on how these and other features of the program affect graduates' sense of preparedness, their career aspirations, and their actual teaching practice. We must also take into account the complex interaction of teacher qualification, program features, and school contexts.

At the same time, the fact that 40% of all teachers in the study did drop out cannot be ignored. This finding is especially worrisome since it includes the high-quality IESP graduates on whom considerable money and effort have been expended. Such high rates are disruptive and harmful as institutional memory is lost and resources are squandered on training and preparing more teachers. Moreover, if the teachers who leave are stronger than those who replace them, the effect of turnover is definitely distressing.

Also disturbing is the finding that, compared to other teachers, IESP graduates have a greater likelihood of leaving the public system for the private school sector after fulfilling their scholarship requirements. This should serve as a warning to policy makers and the Ministry of Education which has invested large sums of money in the program. Israel's private education sector offers more opportunities for excellence and entrepreneurship, which can be attractive to bright teachers. At the same time, the public establishment has invested large sums in the IESP project and has faith in its potential to improve the public educator workforce.

Although a variety of factors influence attrition, the emphasis here is on job satisfaction and motivation to leave the teaching profession. It seems encouraging that IESP teachers are not less satisfied compared to their counterparts. It seems that teachers' perceptions of school quality and context are strongly linked to teacher job satisfaction. Like most other workers, teachers form their opinions and make decisions about their schools based on their personal beliefs and expectations as well as the quality of their working conditions (Ladd, 2011).

Although it is possible to measure aspects of school context more objectively, the current study tapped teachers' perceptions of their school's quality. This was the most effective predictor of job satisfaction, better than many other personal and organizational factors that were examined. Thus the main conclusion to emerge from this study is clear and unambiguous: what teachers perceive as quality working conditions is highly predictive of individual teacher job satisfaction.

All the same, this finding must be interpreted with care since the study did not indicate what specific attributes IESP teachers look for in a school. Is it the composition of the students, the leadership of the principal, the ethos and vision of the school, its reputation and public status? Answers to these questions should be examined in the future.

A second predictor of teacher job satisfaction was the quality of new teacher induction. Considerable evidence suggests that comprehensive induction influences teacher retention (Bickmore & Bickmore, 2010; Wang, Odell; & Schwille, 2008). This study reinforces the finding that systematic induction, embedded in a healthy school climate, contributes to teachers' job satisfaction.

Advocates of programs to recruit academically talented candidates into teaching may be encouraged by the early findings that IESP teachers neither left teaching more frequently than less academically able teachers, nor were less satisfied working as teachers. Furthermore, IESP candidates wanted to become teachers from the beginning and chose teaching as a career more frequently than other teachers. This may imply that IESP graduates are more idealistic and committed to teaching than other teachers.

Unfortunately, core features of the teaching profession make it difficult to increase the selectivity of the teaching workforce in Israel. Such factors include the large number of teachers needed, the low salary, the absence of a career ladder, limited status, and organizational authority. Still, the IESP is succeeding in recruiting bright candidates, training them for teaching and proving that they do not leave teaching more frequently than other teachers.

It is noteworthy that the IESP teachers' reasons for dropping out differ from their counterparts. IESP teachers differentiate between working with the children *inside* the classroom which they enjoy and the day-to-day working conditions *outside* the classroom such as the low salary and the broader educational system, which they criticize. In general, job satisfaction is a function of the balance between rewards and challenges provided by the job and the expected or desired rewards sought by the individual.

Employees' frames of reference for evaluating their working conditions are a function of the alternatives available (Stanley et al., 2013; Trevor, 2001). Trevor hypothesizes that education and cognitive ability affect the alternatives available to workers, functioning as "movement capital" in the labor market (see also Bretz, Boudreau, & Judge, 1994). We can therefore interpret job dissatisfaction among IESP teachers in light of their "movement capital," which affects their perceptions of the challenges and difficulties in the school environment.

Even though they enjoy teaching, teaching may not hold them. IESP teachers may resent the low salary and flaws of the educational system because they are more sensitive to and critical of systemic problems. Although higher salaries may mitigate some criticism, collective agreements of Israel's teachers' union do not permit such a policy. It is likely that more IESP teachers could be retained in the public school system if the program focused not only on recruitment incentives but also on continuing support and development of new teachers.

If we want to recruit and retain highly qualified candidates to the teaching profession, we need to understand better what kind of induction and ongoing professional development they need. Professionalization depends on a knowledgeable, skilled, well-regarded work force with a high degree of organizational authority and resource control (Goldstein, 2007). Changing the composition of the workforce through staffing reforms may improve the status of the teaching profession, but do little to professionalize teaching.

By contrast, strengthening induction and professional development should increase teachers' knowledge and skills. This could lead to greater teacher authority over school-wide decisions and lay the basis for a genuine career ladder. Reforms that address such elements of professionalization may alter the perspectives of academically talented teachers toward teaching and help alleviate their discontent. Hopefully, such policies will increase the retention of our best and brightest teachers.

To inform efforts to improve the IESP, future research should consider at least three questions. First, what elements of teacher preparation and socialization are most critical for preparing excellent candidates who maintain their commitment to teaching? Second, what organizational and structural changes in the public schools might increase the job satisfaction of academically able teachers? Third, what school leadership practices and career ladder opportunities help such teachers succeed over time? Answers to these questions can help recruit, nurture, and retain an elite cadre of educators in Israel and other countries.

NOTES

1. This analysis is part of a larger evaluation study of the IESP focused on graduates' integration into teaching, aspirations and professional development, and perceptions of the program (Libman, 2013).
2. The small number of Arab IESP graduates in the sample may make this finding unreliable.

REFERENCES

Bickmore, D. L., & Bickmore, S. T. (2010). A multifaceted approach to teacher induction. *Teaching & Teacher Education, 26*, 1006–1014.

Borman, G. D., & Dowling, M. N. (2008). Teacher attrition and retention: A meta-analysis and narrative review of the research. *Review of Educational Research, 78*(3), 367–409.

Boyd, D., Grossman, P., Lankford, H., Loeb, S., & Wyckoff, J. (2009). Teacher preparation and student achievement. *Educational Evaluation and Policy Analysis, 31*, 416–440.

Bretz, R. D., Boudreau, J. W., & Judge, T. A. (1994). Job search behavior of employed managers. *Personnel Psychology, 47*, 275–301.

Clotfelter, C., Ladd, H., & Vigdor, J. (2010). Teacher credentials and student achievement in high school: A cross-subject analysis with student fixed effect. *Journal of Human Resources, 45*, 655–681.

European Union. (2013). *Study on policy measures to improve the attractiveness of the teaching profession in Europe*. Final Report (Volumes 1 & 2). Luxembourg: Publications Office of the European Union. http://ec.europa.eu/education/news/2014/2010428-teaching-profession-attractive_en.htm.

Goldstein, J. (2007). Easy to dance to: Solving the problems of teacher evaluation with peer assistance and review. *American Journal of Education, 113*, 479–508.

Henry, G. T., Bastian, K. C., & Smith, A. A. (2012). Scholarship to recruit the "Best and brightest" into teaching: Who is recruited, where do they teach, how effective are they, and how long do they stay? *Educational Researcher, 41*(3), 83–92.

Ingersoll, R. (2001). Teacher turnover and teacher shortages: An organizational analysis. *American Educational Research Journal, 38*, 499–534.

Ladd, H. F. (2011). Teachers' perceptions of their working conditions: How predictive of planned and actual teacher movement. *Educational Evaluation and Policy Analysis, 32*(2), 235–261.

Lankford, H., Loeb, S., McEachin, A., Miller, L. C., & Wyckoff, J. (2014). Who enters teaching? Encouraging evidence that the status of teaching is improving. *Educational Researcher, 49*(9), 444–453.

Libman, Z. (2014). Overqualification and teacher retention: The case of the excellent students' project graduates. *Gilui Daat, 5*, 41–64.

Libman, Z., Ackerman-Asher, H., & Maskit, D. (2013). The project for excellent students: An evaluation report. Research Report. Tel-Aviv: Ministry of Education, Israel.

OECD. (2011). *Teachers matter: Attracting, developing and retaining effective teachers: Pointers for policy development*. Directorate for Education, Education and Training Policy Division, OECD. Retrieved from: http://www.oecd.org/edu/school/48627229.pdf.

Stanley, L., Vandenberghe, C., Vandenberg, R. & Bentein, K. (2013). Commitment profiles and employee turnover. *Journal of Vocational Behavior, 82,* 176–187.

Trevor, C. O. (2001). Interactions among actual ease-of-movement determinants and job satisfaction in the prediction of voluntary turnover. *Academy of Management Journal, 44,* 621–638.

Wang, J., Odell, S. J., & Schwille, S. A. (2008). Effects of teacher induction on beginning teachers' training: A critical review of literature. *Journal of Teacher Education, 59*(2), 132–152.

Xu, Z., Hannaway, J., & Taylor, C. (2011). Making a difference? The effects of Teach For America in high school. *Journal of Policy Analysis & Management, 30,* 447–469.

Chapter Six

Centering Teacher Education on High-Leverage Practices

Francesca M. Forzani

Over the past decade, a small but growing number of teacher educators have begun working to refocus initial teacher education directly on specific teaching practices—often referred to as "core" or "high-leverage" practices (Forzani, 2014; Grossman, Hammerness, & McDonald, 2009; McDonald, Kazemi, & Kavanagh, 2013; Windshitl, Thompson, Braaten, & Stroupe, 2012). This has typically involved marshaling some consensus within a teacher education program around a set of teaching practices that are considered essential for responsible novice teaching, and offering students repeated opportunities to practice them to the point of competency, with close coaching and feedback.

Although high-leverage practices (HLPs) include lesson planning, assessment, and other elements of teaching that do not involve direct interaction with students, many of these efforts have focused on interactive instructional practices such as leading discussions, conferencing with students, and implementing classroom routines. One of the primary goals is to establish a common and specific standard of competence and hold teacher educators and their students accountable for reaching that standard.

High-leverage-practices-focused teacher education is one of several recent efforts to develop professional training focused directly on novices' learning the work of teaching rather than on traditional academic or theoretical topics with limited relevance to the classroom realities. Other practice-based initiatives include extending the length of student teaching and other kinds of field experiences and creating teacher residencies that situate most of novices' learning in K-12 classrooms. All these efforts aim to prepare teachers who are skilled at teaching, not just at studying and analyzing schools; however, the high-leverage-practices approach is distinct in its focus on rebuilding the curriculum around specific practices.

This chapter offers a definition of high-leverage practices and high-leverage practices-based teacher education and provides a rationale for the approach. It draws examples from TeachingWorks and from the undergraduate elementary teacher education program at the University of Michigan, where teacher educators have been collaborating for nearly a decade to identify high-leverage practices and to develop approaches to teacher training.

WHY HIGH-LEVERAGE PRACTICES?

Unlike many other fields of professional work, teaching lacks consensus about the practices necessary for competent beginning performance. Nor is there a common, technical language for describing and analyzing those practices in ways that make them accessible for novices' learning.

Many states and professional organizations have created general performance standards for new teachers that describe broad domains of competence—usually lesson planning, employing a variety of instructional strategies to meet the needs of different students, managing the classroom, assessing learning, and working with parents, caregivers, and colleagues. Still there is no agreement about the specific practices within those domains that new teachers should be able to carry out in order to perform their work responsibly.

This lack of a detailed articulation of practice and shared, professional language has impeded the development of teacher education into effective professional training. It is hard to offer the kind of modeling and close coaching so common in professional education in other fields in the absence of well-specified performance standards. Suchy training also depends on video exemplars or other curriculum materials that help define competent practice.

Instead, the preservice curriculum focuses on lesson planning and other "pre-active" elements of the work and on educational psychology and the social and financial contexts of schooling rather than on the actual work of teaching (Ball & Forzani, 2009). Many such programs rely on student teaching or other field placements to help students learn to teach, without specifying in detail what they should learn to do while they are working in classrooms or holding them accountable for whether they learn it.

Similarly, most licensure examinations measure general knowledge for teaching, and only rarely evaluate candidates on their ability to carry out specific instructional practices such as leading discussions or designing tests and quizzes. Solving these problems depends on developing a common and

detailed understanding of the specific practices needed for responsible beginning teaching.

DEFINING HIGH-LEVERAGE PRACTICES AND HLP-BASED TEACHER EDUCATION

High-leverage practices are basic teaching tasks used with high frequency
from a teacher's first day on the job. Such tasks cannot be delegated to
another teacher or school professional. They are critical to teaching worthwhile content; consequential for students' social, emotional, and intellectual
development in school; and generative of future learning on the teacher's
part.

High-leverage practices are useful across a broad range of subject areas,
grade levels, and teaching contexts. They are "high-leverage" because they
are closely linked to student learning and also because if a teacher can use
them well, he or she will be able to implement many different kinds of
curricula and teaching strategies and be well prepared to develop more advanced skills.

High-leverage-practices-based teacher education makes the learning of
HLPs the core goal of the curriculum for learning to teach. This means that
instructional activities, field experiences, and assessments are directly focused on helping students learn the skills and techniques to carry out specific
practices and the knowledge, judgment, and commitments required to carry
them out responsibly and flexibly, in response to specific pupils' needs.

If teachers are going to use an HLP like leading group discussion of
literary texts, they need to understand how students are likely to understand
those texts, what they will find interesting and confusing, how best to sequence the questions they will pose, and how to label and organize the work
students will do in the discussion. They also need to understand and appreciate students' varied linguistic backgrounds and be able to draw on and
respond to them during the discussion, so that all students know how to
contribute productively and no one is shut out because of cultural norms for
talking.

One can think about a high-leverage-practices-based curriculum in terms
of the three strands reflected in the example above:

1. *Instructional practices* (e.g., leading whole group discussions), focuses on the actual work teachers do, including high-leverage practices and their components, and other techniques and skills of teaching;
2. *Content knowledge for teaching* focuses on the special ways that
   teachers need to understand the content they are going to teach;

3. *Professional and practical foundations* focuses on educational history and policy, and learning, culture, and context, as they affect students' opportunities to learn, and on professional ethics, including teachers' obligations to work assiduously to meet all students' needs.

In this model, high-leverage practices are not only the focus of the instructional practices strand, but the source of the other two strands: Content knowledge for teaching and professional and practical foundational knowledge are necessary to carry out high-leverage practices. Although aspiring teachers might study many interesting and relevant topics and issues, teacher education is generally too short to be spent on something unrelated to carrying out high-leverage practices.

Much of the work on HLP-focused teacher education has focused on designing the instructional practice strand of the curriculum. The limited but growing literature on this work reflects an emerging consensus that an effective instructional practice strand has four features: (1) a clear focus on specific high-leverage practices; (2) pedagogies specially developed to teach HLPs, such as modeling, video analysis, and rehearsal (e.g., Lampert et al., 2013; McDonald, Kazemi, & Kavanagh, 2013); (3) classroom settings, including K-12 settings, deliberately designed for learning practice; and (4) assessments focused on the HLPs (Ball & Forzani, 2009). The hallmark of this approach is the deliberate focus on specific teaching practices, which are made clear to students from the outset of a program or course and are targeted in core assignments and program completion requirements.

IDENTIFYING HIGH-LEVERAGE PRACTICES: AN EXAMPLE FROM TEACHINGWORKS

TeachingWorks, an organization that develops materials and approaches for practice-based teacher education, has identified and specified a comprehensive list of high-leverage practices (see Table 6.1). Although this is not the only or even the best list of practices, it helps illustrate the concept of an HLP and the considerations that have to be weighed in any effort to identify HLPs or core practices.

The work began by defining the ideas that undergird the organization's vision of good teaching and learning. Because there are far more teaching practices that conform to this vision than can be covered in most initial teacher education programs, criteria were developed for choosing elements of practice most important for beginners. Finally, strategic decisions were made about the grain size for representing the practices.

Table 6.1. TeachingWorks High-Leverage Practices

1.	Leading a group discussion
2.	Explaining and modeling content, practices, and strategies
3.	Eliciting and interpreting individual students' thinking
4.	Diagnosing particular common patterns of student thinking and development in a subject-matter domain
5.	Implementing norms and routines for classroom discourse and work
6.	Coordinating and adjusting instruction during a lesson
7.	Specifying and reinforcing productive student behavior
8.	Implementing organizational routines
9.	Setting up and managing small group work
10.	Building respectful relationships with students
11.	Talking about a student with parents or other caregivers
12.	Learning about students' cultural, religious, family, intellectual, and personal experiences and resources for use in instruction
13.	Setting long- and short-term learning goals for students
14.	Designing single lessons and sequences of lessons
15.	Checking student understanding during and at the conclusion of lessons
16.	Selecting and designing formal assessments of student learning
17.	Interpreting the results of student work, including routine assignments, quizzes, tests, projects, and standardized assessments
18.	Providing oral and written feedback to students
19.	Analyzing instruction for the purpose of improving it

(TeachingWorks, 2015)

FIVE CORE IDEAS ABOUT TEACHING AND LEARNING

Five core convictions undergird the TeachingWorks HLPs:

1. *The goal of classroom teaching is to help students learn worthwhile knowledge and skills and develop the ability to use what they learn for their own purposes.* Worthwhile knowledge and skills refers to the big ideas that have contributed to the cultures, political systems, economies, and problems of the twenty-first century, and high-level thinking, reasoning, and problem-solving skills. School should equip students to analyze texts critically, compose persuasive arguments and execute them effectively both orally and in writing, and use skills of scientific analysis and mathematical reasoning to understand and re-

spond to complex problems. It should also help them appreciate others' perspectives and be able to challenge and build on them effectively using a range of tools. This includes studying the ideas, histories, and literatures of peoples and cultures excluded from dominant narratives and socio-political systems.

2. *All students deserve the opportunity to learn at high levels.* All students have the capacity to learn. Teachers are obligated to work assiduously to ensure equitable access to worthwhile learning and opportunities for personal development.

3. *Learning is an active sense-making process.* The process of learning, particularly the learning of challenging material, is an active and interactive one on the part of students. The deepest and most lasting understanding and skill to come about as students encounter new ideas and skills, try them out, consider feedback from both the teacher and their peers and try again, and listen to and observe similar attempts by their classmates. Rather than receiving new information passively or magically developing skills by watching others demonstrate them, students learn and grow through active sense making and through practice.

4. *Teaching is interactive work, co-constructed with students.* Teaching that helps students learn worthwhile knowledge and skills is not the direct transmission of ideas to students, but strategic work to facilitate interactions between and among the teacher and what he or she knows, the students and what they know and can do, and the content being taught (Cohen, Raudenbush, & Ball, 2003). Skillful teaching deploys practices and techniques to ensure that students' encounters with academic content and their efforts to learn it are appropriate, organized, and effective.

5. *The contexts of classroom teaching matter, and teachers must manage and use them well.* The work that teachers and students do together in classrooms is influenced and sometimes determined by the school and local communities and by both local and national educational and policy contexts. Consequently, teachers must manage the influence of broader environments on teaching and learning and use those contexts as resources for instruction.

These ideas informed the selection of potential high-leverage practices. To engage students in demanding intellectual work and support the learning of worthwhile content and skills, for example, teachers need facility with such practices as leading group discussions and setting up and managing small group work. To help all students learn, teachers must know how to learn about students' backgrounds and be skilled in unpacking and representing content in ways that make sense to a range of learners. To use and respond effectively to resources and requirements from outside the classroom, such as curriculum frameworks and standardized tests, teachers should be skilled at interpreting the results of student work and setting goals for student learning.

Narrowing the List

TeachingWorks developed and used the following criteria to narrow down what was originally a long list of practices:

1. Occurs with high frequency from a teacher's first day on the job
2. Cannot be delegated by a first-year teacher to another school professional
3. Useful across subject-areas, grade levels, curricula, and instructional approaches
4. Can be unpacked and taught to beginners
5. Are generative of additional learning and skill development
6. Can be assessed

These criteria reflect the exigencies of classroom teaching and teacher education. Teachers often work in different grade levels, with different curricula and instructional approaches, and even in different subject-areas. High-leverage practices must be useful across all these variations. Given the short duration of initial teacher education, HLPs must be essential to beginning teaching. They should be teachable and learnable within the constraints of a typical professional education program, and serve as building blocks for learning more advanced practice.

Finally, HLPs should be assessable so that teacher educators can hold themselves accountable for their graduates' practice. Students should have sufficient opportunity to practice HLPs during initial training and teacher educators should be able to assess them fairly and with reasonable ease.

In formulating HLPs, questions of grain size are extremely important. Practices that are too large may not be treated in appropriate depth, while practices that are too small risk obscuring the larger purposes of instruction. For instance, a practice called "developing a positive classroom culture" is too general to support effective work in a teacher education program unless it is broken down into smaller practices such as implementing routines and supporting productive student behavior.

More finely detailed practices such as asking questions, calling on students, or writing lesson objectives are usually too small. They require little discretionary judgment on the part of the teacher and can easily become disconnected from the broader purposes of instruction. In forming their list, TeachingWorks tried to parse practice at a grain size that maintains the complexity and integrity of teaching but still seems manageable from the perspective of a novice.

DESIGNING A HIGH-LEVERAGE-PRACTICES-BASED TEACHER
EDUCATION PROGRAM:
AN EXAMPLE FROM THE UNIVERSITY OF MICHIGAN

Since 2006, instructors and researchers at the University of Michigan School of Education have collaborated to identify HLPs and redesign their elementary undergraduate teacher education program so that it prepares novices to do the complex work of teaching worthwhile knowledge and skills. Although the redesign effort is a work in progress, it has already achieved many changes that help illustrate what high-leverage, practices-focused teacher education is and does.

The new program is built around three "pillars," corresponding to the three strands of a practice-based curriculum for learning to teach: teaching practice, content knowledge for teaching, and professional ethical obligations (Davis & Boerst, 2014). The "teaching practice strand" helps interns learn to use HLPs, primarily through instructional activities that engage students in deliberate practice of specific elements of teaching. Interns engage in increasingly complex practices over time, often in real K-12 settings, with the gradual fading of scaffolding and support.

The "content knowledge for teaching" strand focuses on the special kinds of knowledge entailed by HLPs and other aspects of teaching (Ball, Thames, & Phelps, 2008), including "knowing what students are likely to understand or misunderstand about specific topics and practices, the affordances and constraints of specific representations of content and practices, and the specialized content knowledge teachers need to guide their instructional decision-making" (Davis & Boerst, 2014, 10). Finally, the "ethical obligations" strand helps interns learn to operationalize nine ethical principles that have been defined by the program, including caring for and demonstrating commitment to every student and ensuring equitable access to learning opportunities.

In all three strands, interns learn in on-campus courses and corresponding field experiences. Both are designed around HLPs or particular elements of content knowledge for teaching. Attention to the ethical obligations of teaching is incorporated throughout. In addition to semester-long courses focused on the knowledge and skill needed to teach a particular subject-area such as mathematics, interns participate in shorter, one- or two-credit courses that address bundles of high-leverage practices.

In *Children as Sense-Makers*, for example, interns learn to elicit and interpret student thinking, implement an appropriate instructional response, define learning goals, model academic content, and assess student learning. In *Teaching with Curriculum Materials,* interns learn to evaluate curriculum materials and select or modify tasks and texts in support of particular learning goals. *Managing to Teach* addresses classroom management skills, including the practices of building relationships with students, giving directions, implementing classroom routines, circulating while students work independently, and using public writing spaces (University of Michigan School of Education, n.d.c.).

Interns are assessed at strategic points throughout the program. An initial series of baseline tests serve as a point of comparison and are followed by mid-program and end-of-program assessments, as well as lower-stakes tests inside of courses (Davis & Boerst, 2014). Many of the assessments hold students directly accountable for demonstrating that they can carry out specific practices effectively. In the eliciting and interpreting student thinking assessment, for example, interns are asked to interview a simulated student to understand his or her thinking in relation to a mathematics problems, drawing on their knowledge of mathematics and of students to construct appropriate questions and probes (Shaughnessy, Sleep, Boerst, & Ball, 2011).

Other assessments require interns to analyze and modify a science lesson plan, provide a clear explanation of a mathematical idea, or give directions for a task (Davis & Boerst, 2014). Rather than rely on proxy measures of interns' capability, such as written analyses of teaching or reflections on student teaching performance, these assessments measure teaching skill directly. Students who do not perform at a satisfactory level receive additional support related to specific practices or content knowledge for teaching.

Faculty members in the University of Michigan elementary undergraduate teacher education program have encountered numerous challenges as they have sought to design a sustainable, HLP-based program that is no more expensive for students or for the program than it was prior to the redesign effort. Some challenges come from the resource- and expertise-intensive work of designing courses that help novices learn to practice. Others come from the demands of administering and reporting on a program that looks different from the norms.

Many challenges are ongoing and require careful shepherding and creativity from a highly committed group of faculty members and other instructors. To manage them, the program has created "foundational frameworks" that make explicit the goals for program redesign and help create institutional memory and orient new members of the teaching staff. New social structures such as a working group to manage the redesign and new tools, such as course design templates have also been created. These tools and structures help the University of Michigan build a teacher education program focused on specific teaching practices and on the knowledge, skills, and orientations needed to carry them out.

THE WORK AHEAD

There is much to learn from the small but growing number of teacher educators and teacher education programs currently exploring HLP-based approaches to the teaching of teaching. The field of teacher education still needs more robust knowledge about which teaching practices are most powerfully linked with pupil learning and the most challenging for novices to learn and use. We also need to understand how certain practices vary across subject-areas, and how to organize and sequence them for novice teachers' learning.

The challenge—and the imperative—is for teacher educators to find ways to talk coherently across different terms for describing teaching, different approaches to defining and identifying HLPs, and different hypotheses about effective methods for teaching teaching. Experimentation is essential, but it must be deliberate in order to achieve the eventual goal of collective understanding and consensus.

NOTE

Many ideas in this chapter were informed by years of conversation and collaboration with the Teacher Education Initiative Curriculum Group at the University of Michigan, staff and students at TeachingWorks at the University of Michigan and members of the Core Practices Consortium. The author gratefully acknowledges Deborah Ball's helpful comments on earlier drafts.

REFERENCES

Ball, D. L., & Forzani, F. M. (2009). The work of teaching and the challenge for teacher education. *Journal of Teacher Education, 60*(5), 497–511.
Ball, D., Thames, M., & Phelps, G. (2008). Content knowledge for teaching: What makes it special? *Journal of Teacher Education, 29*(5), 389–407.
Cohen, D. K., Raudenbush, S., & Ball, D. (2003). Resources, instruction, and research. *Educational Evaluation and Policy Analysis, 25*(2), 1–24.
Davis, B., & Boerst, T. (2014). *Designing elementary teacher education to prepare well-started beginners.* Retrieved from http://www.teachingworks.org/research-data/workingpapers.
Forzani, F. M. (2014). Understanding "core practices" and "practice-based" teacher education: Learning from the past. *Journal of Teacher Education, 65*(4), 357–368.
Grossman, P., Hammerness, K., & McDonald, M. (2009). Redefining teaching, reimagining teacher education. *Teachers and Teaching, 15*(2), 273–289.
Lampert, M., Franke, M. L., Kazemi, E., Ghousseini, H., Turrou, A. C., Beasley, H., Cunard, A., & Crowe, K. (2013). Keeping it complex: Using rehearsals to support novice teacher learning of ambitious teaching. *Journal of Teacher Education, 64*(3), 226–243.
McDonald, M., Kazemi, E., & Kavanagh, S.S. (2013). Core practices and pedagogies of teacher education: A call for a common language and collective activity. *Journal of Teacher Education, 64*(5), 378–386.
TeachingWorks. (2015). *High-leverage practices.* Retrieved from http://www.teachingworks.org/work-of-teaching/high-leverage-practices.

University of Michigan School of Education. (n.d.a.). *EDUC 415. Children as sensemakers.* Retrieved from http://www.soe.umich.edu/academics/courses/EDUC_415/.

University of Michigan School of Education. (n.d.b.). *EDUC 416. Teaching with curriculum materials.* Retrieved from http://www.soe.umich.edu/academics/courses/EDUC_416/.

University of Michigan School of Education. (n.d.c.). *EDUC 414. Managing to teach.* Retrieved from http://www.soe.umich.edu/academics/courses/EDUC_414/.

Windshitl, M., Thompson, J., Braaten, M., & Stroupe, D. (2012). Proposing a core set of instructional practices and tools for teachers of science. *Science Education, 96(5)*, 878–903.

Chapter Seven

Building Teaching Practices Grounded in Foundational Knowledge, Visions, and Contexts

Karen Hammerness and Bill Kennedy

How can teacher educators help new teachers learn to enact teaching practices grounded in values, visions, and contextual knowledge? Preservice programs often provide opportunities for candidates to learn *about* multicultural pedagogies and to read *about* race, class, and culture. But they often fail to link such foundational understandings to specific teaching practices in particular classroom contexts or help teacher candidates learn to use their foundational knowledge in practice.

Growing scholarship on practice-centered teacher education discusses efforts to identify and teach "high-leverage" practices (Forzani, this volume); however, researchers have not fully explored or articulated ways to help new teachers build on and use contextual knowledge and theoretical understandings essential for good teaching. Ideally, teacher education should take an integrated approach to the teaching of theory and practice, situating teacher candidates' learning in a vision of good teaching grounded in specific contexts. Such an approach is consistent with socio-cultural conceptions of learning that emphasize learning in practice and in communities of practice.

These challenges are especially salient in the programs described here which aim to prepare teachers for particular urban contexts where knowledge of learning and contexts is essential to ambitious teaching practice. The University of Chicago Teacher Education Program (UChicago UTEP) prepares teachers for the Chicago Public Schools and the Bard College Master of Arts in Teaching program prepares teachers for New York City public schools. This chapter focuses on the teaching of two core practices: (1) constructing and maintaining democratic classroom communities; and (2) initiating and engaging in critical, reflective dialogue with urban school stakeholders. In both programs, teacher candidates learn these practices through a process of observation, rehearsal, and enactment with feedback, integrated with opportunities to gain relevant foundational and contextual knowledge.

LEARNING TO CONSTRUCT AND MAINTAIN DEMOCRATIC CLASSROOM COMMUNITIES

The Bard Master of Arts in Teaching (MAT) program is a year-long, graduate-level program, coupled with two years of post-program induction support. The program prepares middle and secondary level teachers at the college campus in Annandale-on-Hudson and at an urban residency campus on-site at a high school located in the South Bronx, New York. The MAT program aims to prepare teachers who know their content deeply and who are not only committed to teaching but will stay in the schools that need them the most.

Coursework and curriculum emphasize academic content and pedagogy. Starting in the fall, residency students have a set of internships in different New York City schools—gradually moving from observation, to some teaching experiences, and ultimately to full-time student-teaching. Central to the Bard MAT program's vision is preparing candidates who can design demanding curriculum in their subject area and create democratic classroom learning communities.

To become effective teachers, Bard graduates must learn how to weave individual relationships into a dynamic, learning community. This complex practice requires a broad vision of the kind of classroom community teachers want to create and an understanding of how to construct such a community with students in ways that emphasize respect and a valuing of students as individuals. It involves establishing norms and expectations regarding classroom relationships and behavior, clear routines, and high expectations for quality work. It means creating an environment that reflects students' needs and strengths.

Creating a classroom environment which embodies this democratic perspective is a growing challenge in New York and Chicago schools. In the Bard and UChicago UTEP programs, many graduates find their first teaching positions in public charter and neighborhood schools where a culture of compliance prevails. Pupils are expected to follow rigid behavioral expectations, and obedience-oriented classroom management are commonplace. The reliance on external incentives and the lack of opportunities for student voice, thinking, and creativity undermines the development of an intellectual community and works against deep, engaged learning.

Deconstructing the Practice

In a year-long foundations course called "Contexts of Teaching and Learning in New York City," teacher candidates engage in a series of linked assignments designed to help them learn the practice of creating and maintaining a respectful classroom community informed by foundational and contextual knowledge. The sequence begins with candidates observing the first days of school and then returning six weeks later to study the effects of teachers' actions at the beginning of the school year on classroom culture. The last step involves creating a plan for setting up their own classroom norms and cultures.

Several key concepts and readings inform these linked assignments. Teacher candidates need to understand the concepts of prior knowledge and scaffolding, both ideas from learning theory, in order to create a democratic classroom culture. They also needed to understand the relationship of race, social class, and educational opportunity in order to avoid lowering expectations for low-income children of color.

Three readings support the exploration of these ideas. Jean Anyon's (1980) "Social Class and the Hidden Curriculum of Work," discusses the correlation between intellectual demand and the socio-economic status of children and communities. Martin Haberman's (1991) "Pedagogy of Poverty" describes how pervasive instructional strategies in urban schools communicate lowered expectations for children in poverty. Ron Berger's (2003) chapter "The Radon Project" provides an image of a respectful, democratic classroom where students produce ambitious work and the contributions of all students are valued.

To begin learning the practice of creating a democratic classroom learning community, teacher candidates observe the first three days in their middle and high school placements in order to see what teachers do to set the tone, lay the groundwork for classroom routines and patterns of work and explicitly (or implicitly) initiate a classroom culture. Teacher candidates take fieldnotes, paying attention to questions like these:

> What activities or assignments if any does the teacher use to help students get to know one another? Does the teacher use any activities or assignments to get to know the students as learners, students of the discipline, or individuals? In what ways does the teacher establish routines for the structure of the classroom work, for entering the class and starting work?

Alongside this observational assignment, students read Anyon and Haberman to help them understand how specific ways of creating classroom cultures mirror or challenge the pedagogies of poverty.

The first days of school assignment is paired with a short discussion of learning theory, emphasizing the key ideas of *scaffolding* and *prior knowl-*

edge, which bear on teaching content as well as teaching children how to work together in a learning environment. Just as pupils need scaffolding to learn subject matter, so they also need scaffolding in order to create and participate in a democratic classroom culture. Similarly teachers cannot build on prior knowledge without getting to know their students and what they bring.

From their initial observations, Bard teacher candidates typically notice that some teachers use purposeful scaffolding which stimulates their thinking about the kinds of experiences they could create early on for their future students. They recognize that teachers who establish a few clear routines for beginning and ending the school day seem to move more smoothly through their work with students. Some worry that the specificity of certain routines are too restrictive. This opens up an important conversation about gauging the appropriate level of support. Some teacher candidates observe teachers co-constructing norms for group work, peer editing, or class discussions, which furthers the discussion about democratic approaches to classroom culture.

These observations and the associated readings highlight the ways in which learning opportunities may vary depending on students' social class or school features. Students begin to appreciate the importance of scaffolding student learning without oversimplifying cognitive demands. They classify the different types of school cultures they observe and array classroom routines along two continua—from co-constructed to individually determined and from authoritarian to democratic.

A return visit to the classroom six weeks into the school year helps cement the idea that the strategies teachers use in the beginning of the year have continuing impact over the course of the year. After reviewing notes from their visit in September, teacher candidates observe two class periods, paying particular attention to the classroom environment and the relationships between teacher and students and among the students, and thinking about what the teacher did in the beginning of the year to create such an environment. They also look to see whether norms and routines are in place or have already broken down. This experience helps teacher candidates see and make sense of the work teachers do with students to create a classroom community—work that may be invisible, especially to novices.

Rehearsing the Practice

In the final assignment, students write about the kind of classroom they imagine setting up for children. Then in groups, they develop a lesson plan for introducing one classroom norm at the beginning of the school year, attending to the following questions:

How you will introduce the norm to your students and why it is important?
How will you will model the norm for your students and help them practice it?
How will you assess whether the norm is in place in your classroom?

To make the assignment as realistic as possible, teacher candidates imagine they are planning for the pupils in their mentor's classroom. They study materials from other teachers' classrooms which offer visions of classroom culture and examples of how to scaffold the learning of new routines and expectations. They also read about Ron Berger's "Radon Project." All these examples are deeply rooted in teachers' explicit philosophy of teaching and in foundational concepts of learning.

Teacher candidates practice their lessons in a kind of role play with their classmates. These rehearsals provide an opportunity to test out different ways of introducing norms and to talk through what they might say in their actual classrooms to their own students. Lesson plans are revised based on feedback from peers and the instructor in preparation for trying it out in the mentor's classroom.

In this series of learning experiences, MAT students "deconstruct" the practice of creating democratic classroom communities. They observe how their mentor teachers starts the year with a group of students and what effects the teachers' actions have on classroom culture six weeks into the school year. They read about visions of powerful classroom communities in action and rehearse ways to introduce classroom norms. These learning opportunities are part of a larger conversation about how adolescents learn, including the importance of activating prior knowledge and scaffolding, and how students' experiences in urban schools are shaped by poverty and social class. In this way core teaching practices are connected to foundational ideas about learning and urban contexts.

LEARNING THE PRACTICE OF ENGAGING IN CRITICAL, REFLECTIVE DIALOGUE WITH URBAN SCHOOL STAKEHOLDERS

Housed within the University of Chicago's Urban Education Institute, UChicago UTEP is a two-year Masters in Teaching and Certification program whose mission is to prepare teacher candidates to work in urban public schools. For graduates who choose to work in Chicago Public Schools, UTEP provides three additional years of in-classroom induction coaching. UTEP is neither a traditional, university-based teacher education program nor an alternative certification programs run by a non-profit.

Teacher candidates have multiple, varied clinical experiences in the local context of the city of Chicago, with service experiences in community-based organizations, tutoring and teaching experiences in classrooms, and two different five-month residency placements in Chicago Public School class-rooms. Simultaneous to this extensive clinical experience, candidates take courses on teaching methods commonly found in Chicago Public Schools as well as courses that critically analyze the systemic inequity and oppression operating in the local context, and on a national and global scale. The program aims to prepare teachers who are change agents, reflective practitioners who can teach effectively within the existing local urban system and also improve the system.

Achieving this mission depends on broadening the notion of "teacher educator" beyond the university faculty to include the stakeholders of urban schools that candidates hope to serve. The program defines school stakeholders as students, teachers, non-teaching staff members (e.g., school clerk, janitor, security guard), school administrators, parents, and community members. The voices of these stakeholders—their stories, their opinions about candidates' teaching practice, their ideas about what is worth learning in our candidates' classrooms—are as much a part of the program's curriculum as the voices of UTEP's faculty and staff. Helping teacher candidates learn to initiate and engage all stakeholders in dialogue is a core practice of the program.

The teacher candidates who come to the program often bring some commitment to social justice and a theoretical awareness that teachers working for justice should engage urban school stakeholders in dialogue. But many candidates lack experience talking with any school stakeholders, and nearly all candidates lack experience dialoguing with school stakeholders in Chicago. Therefore, one of the first assignments candidates have when they enter the program is learning to initiate and engage with a variety of school stakeholders in critical, reflective dialogue. Because engaging in dialogue with urban school stakeholders is a complex and nuanced practice, this assignment is the first of several iterations across the two years of the program.

Deconstructing the Practice

Before they begin working on this practice, teacher candidates must become critically conscious of two key approaches to teaching and learning which still dominate American schooling: (1) the teacher is the (sole) holder of knowledge, and (2) didactic learning through transmission is the best pedagogical design. These two approaches maintain a status quo which marginalizes and oppresses poor communities of color, particularly in urban communities, the very communities UTEP prepares teachers to serve.

Developing a critical consciousness about these approaches at this early stage in teacher preparation is crucial since these approaches can be reconfirmed for candidates at every turn. Many candidates also report that their own schooling experience was dominated by these approaches to teaching and learning, which they see in their clinical placements. Furthermore graduates of the program continue to report that they are encouraged or required by school stakeholders to uphold these approaches in their own practice.

Much of the work described here takes place in a year-long Guided Fieldwork course in the first year of the program. Like the Bard program, UChicago UTEP uses Jean Anyon's "Social Class and the Hidden Curriculum of Work" as well as selections from Ira Shor's "Empowering Education" as frames for preparing candidates to analyze urban schooling and to see the ways that schools and their curriculum reproduce the status quo of American society.

These readings and their associated discussions help candidates begin to critically examine the curriculum in schools they will visit, for example to see if those students are asked to engage in rote memorization and lower-order thinking, or if there are opportunities for students to engage in the higher-order, creative, inquiry curriculum most often found in schools whose student population comes from elite or economically advantaged families and communities. This frame for analyzing curriculum is complemented by readings in two other courses, which focus on the legacy of the intersection between Chicago economic policy and Chicago Public School policy (Lipman, 2002; Payne, 2008) and national and international economic and school policy (Labaree, 1997).

Once candidates are more critically conscious of the dominant approach to schooling, they begin to see a purpose for a more dialogic approach to teaching and learning. We support their curiosity with reading and discussion of culturally relevant pedagogy (Ladson-Billings, 1995) and a "funds of knowledge" approach (Moll, Amanti, Neff, & Gonzalez, 1992) to teaching, which claims that teachers must understand the knowledge and experiences of their students, their families, and the communities in order to help them become academically successful. Candidates are also introduced to the idea—through a critical race theory lens—that urban school stakeholders are valuable, that they have important stories to tell, and that they are potential partners in the endeavor of educating urban children.

Rehearsing the Practice

The first step of rehearsal is for candidates to join one of six "Stakeholder Dialogue Groups" organized around the stakeholders typically found at a neighborhood school—administrators, teachers, non-teaching staff, students, parents, and community members. Candidates brainstorm assets and concerns that each stakeholder group might bring to their experience in an urban neighborhood school in the Chicago Public Schools.

This brainstorm tends to surface deficit perspectives that teacher candidates have toward students, families, and communities living and going to school in economically divested neighborhoods of color. The brainstorm also provides opportunities to share asset knowledge and understanding of these same stakeholders that sometimes comes from personal or professional experience. This mix of perspectives in the cohort is *intentional* and reflects the program's recruitment strategy. UTEP makes a concerted effort to draw candidates from the local context, specifically college graduates who attended Chicago Public Schools or have lived and worked in or with Chicago schools and communities. The knowledge and perspectives of these candidates helps shape the early stakeholder conversations in ways that enrich the assigned foundational readings.

Each week, throughout the first year of the program, an instructor leads the cohort—grouped into six stakeholder dialogue groups—on guided visits to different neighborhood elementary (K-8) schools in intentionally chosen neighborhoods across the city of Chicago. All groups consider the following essential question: "What is/isn't typical about Chicago Public Schools?" Each school visit lasts two to three hours and follows a prearranged routine organized around three core experiences: (a) school tour/classroom visits, (b) presentation by the school principal, and (c) the centerpiece—stakeholder dialogues. The school tour and principal presentation are opportunities for the candidates to observe the school communities firsthand, albeit only briefly and often in ways that feel performative on the schools' part and allow candidates to remain passive consumers.

The third core experience—the Stakeholder Dialogues—require *active participation* from the candidates. Each group, made up of four to five UChicago UTEP teacher candidates, sits down in a circle for an hour with three to five stakeholders from said stakeholder groups (e.g., the "Parent" group of four to five candidates talks with four to five parents from the school we visit that day; the following week, that same group of UChicago UTEP candidates sits with a new group of parents at the new school we are visiting). As teacher candidates walk the halls of different Chicago Public Schools and dialogue with members of those schools and communities, they see how policies impact different racial and economic groups within a large urban system.

For example, teacher candidates see the ways that school racial populations can be interpreted as a reflection of the decades of housing policies in the city. Very few schools have demographics that represent a mix of races, and most schools in CPS are populated by only one race. Another example that becomes obvious to teacher candidates through dialogue with school stakeholders is the economic disparity between schools in middle-class neighborhoods and schools in poor neighborhoods. Even though the system allocates the same dollar amount per pupil to all schools in CPS, schools in middle-class neighborhoods supplement that allocation through additional fundraising. These experiences raise candidates' critical consciousness, a hallmark of the programs' beliefs and practices of a critical pedagogy in both teacher education and K-12 classrooms.

The rehearsal of this practice of initiating and engaging in critical reflective dialogue with school stakeholders is most explicit and intentional in this year-long guided Fieldwork course. However, there are at least two other instances in the second year of the program, where teacher candidates have new opportunities to rehearse this practice—as residents prepare to enter their first placement, and again as they prepare to enter their second placement.

One of the first major classroom-based tasks that second-year residents complete is a "Community Ethnography" of their residency site. As a team, four to five residents at a school site engage in a series of tasks that include initiating and engaging in dialogue with school stakeholders. UTEP staff no longer guide this task as they did in the first year of the program. Instead, teams must draw on the skills they learned to seek out school stakeholders who may or may not be expecting to engage in dialogue with teacher candidates working in their building or in their community. Working as a team allows teacher candidates to support one another as they encounter new and unexpected challenges to this practice.

Residents again engage in this practice when they enter their second residency placement in January of the second year. This time, residents are often placed at residency sites by themselves, so they must initiate and engage in these dialogues with school stakeholders by themselves.

With each rehearsal of this practice of initiating and engaging in dialogue, the candidates engage in a critical praxis; first reflecting on the new experiences with urban school stakeholder dialogue, then identifying areas for improvement, reconnecting to the theories they read in the first-year courses, coming up with a plan of action, and finally implementing that plan. This plan can be any number of steps that make sense in that context at that moment for the teacher candidate. For example, a teacher candidate might collaborate with their supervising teacher to reach out to parents by telephone or through home visits. If the teacher candidate realizes they know very little about the surrounding community, she might make a plan to attend some community events or connect with community-based organizations near the school. These residency experiences help prepare candidates for their first year of teaching.

PRACTICES CENTRAL TO THE SUCCESS OF EARLY TEACHERS

These two teaching practices—*constructing and maintaining democratic classroom communities* and *initiating and engaging in critical reflective dialogue with urban school stakeholders*—could be considered part of an initial repertoire for novice teachers to learn to enact (Feiman-Nemser, 2001). While these practices are not typical instructional practices, like orchestrating a classroom discussion or managing group work, they are just as central to the early success of new urban teachers. The two programs featured here move beyond teaching candidates *about* these practices, and into opportunities to deconstruct, rehearse, and enact these practices (Grossman et al., 2009). At the same time the practices are taught in relation to foundational ideas and in the context of a broader vision of good teaching.

These experiences demonstrate how teacher education programs cultivate a vision of good teaching while teaching specific practices that reflect and represent that vision. In teaching these two practices, the Bard MAT program and UChicago UTEP try simultaneously to help new teachers maintain and strengthen their visions of good teaching by focusing on a set of specific and complex practices consistent with that vision. Program faculty and staff work to teach these practices while simultaneously moving between vision and practice and between concrete action and theory. They also teach these practices in relation to theoretical ideas that help candidates understand their underlying purpose and tie them to specific enactments in their own teaching contexts.

The Bard course provides multiple opportunities for teacher candidates to read powerful visions of classroom communities, to articulate their own visions of the kind of classrooms they sought to create, and to learn foundational and theoretical ideas that can ground and support those visions. Teacher candidates observe, deconstruct, and rehearse practices related to creating a democratic learning community in relation to a vision of good teaching and a set of specific foundational ideas. At UChicago UTEP, the program provides multiple opportunities to develop teachers' commitments to social justice and a vision of teachers as change agents in relation to key foundational ideas about race and equity, culturally relevant pedagogy and funds of knowledge. Then in carefully selected and contrasting school contexts, candidates learn and rehearse the specific practice of initiating and engaging in critical reflective dialogue with urban stakeholders.

Longitudinal research finds that graduates from both UChicago UTEP and Bard remain in the urban settings for which they were prepared longer than most novice teachers (Tamir, 2013). Perhaps learning some concrete practices that are theoretically based and consistent with teacher candidates' visions of good teaching enables graduates to feel a sense of success in building relationships with their students, families, co-workers, the administration, and community members.

REFERENCES

Anyon, J. (1980). Social class and the hidden curriculum of work. *The Journal of Education, 162*(1), 67–92.

Ball, D., & Forzani, F. (2009). The work of teaching and the challenge for teacher education. *Journal of Teacher Education, 60*(5), 497–511.

Berger, R. (2003). *An ethic of excellence: Building a culture of craftsmanship with students.* New York: Heinemann.

Feiman Nemser, S. (2001). From preparation to practice: Designing a continuum to strengthen and sustain teaching. *Teachers College Record, 103*(6), 1013–1055.

Grossman, P., K. Hammerness, & McDonald, M. (2009). Redefining teaching, reimagining teacher education. *Teachers and Teaching: Theory and Practice, 15*(2), 273–289.

Haberman, M. (1991). The pedagogy of poverty. *Phi Delta Kappan, 73*(4), 290–294.

Labaree, D. F. (1997). Public goods, private goods: The American struggle over educational goals. *American Educational Research Journal, 34*(1), 39–81.

Ladson-Billings, G. (1995). Toward a theory of culturally relevant pedagogy. *American Educational Research Journal, 32*(3), 465–491.

Lipman, P. (2002). Making the global city, making inequality: The political economy and cultural politics of Chicago school policy. *American Educational Research Journal, 39*(2), 379–419.

Moll, L. C., Amanti, C., Neff, D., & Gonzalez, N. (1992). Funds of knowledge for teaching: Using a qualitative approach to connect homes and classrooms. *Theory into Practice, 31*(2), 132–141.

Payne, C. (2008). *So much reform, so little change: The persistence of failure in urban schools.* Cambridge, MA: Harvard Education Press.

Shor, I. (2012). *Empowering education: Critical teaching for social change.* Chicago: University of Chicago Press.

Tamir, E. (2013). What keeps teachers in and what drives them out: How urban public, urban Catholic, and Jewish day schools affect beginning teachers' careers. *Teachers College Record, 115*(6), 1–36.

Chapter Eight

Building an Urban Teacher Residency in a Third Space Partnership

Monica Taylor and Emily J. Klein

In the fall of 2009, the Dean of the College of Education and Human Services at Montclair State University invited the authors and a third faculty member to re-imagine what teacher education could look like. In response to a Teacher Quality Partnership grant from the U.S. Department of Education's Office of Innovation and Improvement, she charged the faculty team to create a math and science teacher residency program in collaboration with the College's longtime partner, the Newark Public Schools. The resulting urban teacher residency program blends knowledge from the university and from the schools to create a "third space" serving the needs of all parties involved.

The defining feature of an urban teacher residency is an extended apprenticeship in a school with a highly skilled mentor teacher (Solomon, 2009). Coursework is often intertwined with residents' classroom experiences, and an induction program usually supports teachers in their first years of teaching. Research on urban residency programs indicates higher retention rates for graduates compared with graduates from traditional teacher education programs and documents the benefits of the extended and intensive fieldwork component (Papay, West, Fullerton, & Kane, 2012).

From the start, the Newark Montclair Urban Teacher Residency (NMUTR), and in particular the math/science secondary program, rested on a unique and radical vision of teacher education. Drawing from the fields of cultural studies, post-colonial theory, geography, and critical literacy (Bhabha, 1994), it was conceptualized as a third space, a hybrid program located between the institutional partners, that was continually being negotiated and constructed.

Building this residency required educators from the district, school, and university to think differently about teacher education. Combining the strengths of these individuals and their respective institutions led to an entirely new program that was neither led by the university (first space) nor the schools (second space) but existed in a third space that was always being negotiated. The residency became a hybrid space that embraced the essential elements of both institutions while inviting the creation of new features, practices, and tools.

Those involved had to re-imagine their roles in teacher education and develop new ideas about how to prepare urban teachers and foster teacher leadership and school change. For instance, mentor teachers do not customarily develop curriculum for university courses and university faculty do not teach in high school classrooms. Could these traditional boundaries be crossed? Creating a third space required ongoing, generative conversations among all participants to determine roles and responsibilities, common goals/objectives, instructional strategies, assignments, and assessment tools. It was a difficult and time-consuming process that required constant tending.

The guiding vision was to prepare urban teachers who would develop socially just, inquiry-based practices. This meant challenging deficit stereotypes of urban youth and creating a teacher education curriculum that enabled residents to develop more complex, sociocultural portraits of their students and their communities. Teaching *about* culturally responsive teaching was not enough. Residents needed to reflect on their own identities and develop authentic relationships with Newark youth so that they could begin to think about teaching from a "funds of knowledge" perspective (Gonzalez, Moll, & Amanti, 2005). Hopefully this would lead to classrooms where students were active constructors of knowledge, working alongside teachers to pose and solve problems in the world (Dewey, 1916; Freire, 1970).

NMUTR SECONDARY COHORT PROGRAM FRAMEWORK

Residents enter the program with an undergraduate degree in a math or science field that met New Jersey's content area certification requirements. Most residents live in New Jersey. Some were recent college graduates; others were more seasoned change-of-career candidates. They bring varying degrees of professional experience and experience in urban contexts.

During the twelve-month program, residents receive a $26,000 stipend as well as free tuition for a Masters of Teaching from Montclair State University. In exchange, they are asked to complete three years of teaching in Newark with induction support provided by the university. Additionally they receive support and guidance in seeking certification and a teaching position in the district.

The program begins in June with an intensive week-long course at MSU, co-taught by three faculty. Residents reflect on their own learning experiences, analyzed learning theories, unpacked issues of identity and social justice, and developed goals for the summer. In the second week, residents participate in a professional development workshop on inquiry-based learning led by the staff at the Newark Museum, one of the community partners. Then they teach science and math units at the summer camps at the Newark Museum and La Casa De Don Pedro, and serve as "relationship managers" for urban youth participating in the Newark All Stars internship.

In August, residents meet with their mentor teachers to map curriculum and design lesson plans for the upcoming school year. Together they set up their classrooms and attended school-wide professional development workshops. On the first day of school, mentors and residents greet their students as co-teachers. Residents then spend the next ten months completely immersed in their Newark public school communities. Once a week, they meet with university faculty for a three-hour class held at one of several schools.

During the regular school year, mentors participate in all aspects of the program including curriculum development, observations, and evaluation. The third space design team created new processes for writing and reviewing lesson plans, conducting informal and formal observations, and ultimately evaluating the residents. The lesson plan format scaffolds the kinds of thinking that the mentors and faculty valued for instruction. As the fall semester progresses, residents present their lesson plans for review. The structured process allows mentors, residents, and faculty to provide constructive feedback aimed at promoting inquiry-oriented teaching.

New structures for observing and debriefing residents' teaching are also used. Observers script lessons, focusing on the exchanges between resident and students. These scripts provide a basis for mentors and faculty to engage in rich discussions about residents' lessons, based in records of practice, rather than personal judgements or assumptions.

A modified version of "Reformed Teaching Observation Protocol" (Piburn et al., 2000) provides a framework for instructional rounds. Developed at Arizona State University for observing constructivist math and science inquiry teaching, this tool helps residents observe, reflect, and refine their teaching practices. In the fall, rounds focus on mentors' teaching; in the spring, the focus switches to residents' teaching. Having different faculty conduct these observations provides residents with varied perspectives on their practice.

During the spring, residents participate in a series of workshops that helped them examine learning needs and modify instruction for English language learners and students with disabilities. They also carry out an action research project and a social justice inquiry project. The year ends with residents presenting artifacts reflecting their growth and learning over the year. During the last months of the school year, residents prepare for the job market by writing resumes and educational philosophy statements, participating in mock interviews, and debriefing the job application process.

USING "FUNDS OF KNOWLEDGE" TO TEACH FOR SOCIAL JUSTICE

> Although my family has grown up in Newark and I spent a lot of time there growing up, I am only beginning to understand what it means to be a part of an urban community and the challenges that people face as well as some of the intricacies that make it so beautiful. (Resident, 2013)

The first summer was designed to disrupt preconceived notions about urban youth that residents brought to the program and to help them develop more complex ways of thinking about their students. Even though many residents have suitable pre-dispositions for urban teaching, they still hold problematic assumptions about urban youth, which surfaced in early teaching experiences. Combatting these stereotypes is critical to a social justice foundation for teaching.

The goal is for residents to recognize curriculum and assessment practices that perpetuate and increase social inequities and to create curricula that give students opportunities to find their voices and examine issues of power in society. Clearly a year-long program can only lay a foundation for such work. Additional support for socially just teaching would be needed during the early years of teaching.

From the start, residents participate in a variety of learning experiences designed to help them begin developing a listen to teach habit of mind. Developing such a disposition enables residents to learn to construct curricula that bridges their students' needs and interests and the essential questions, skills, knowledge, and understanding of their content areas.

For example, before the first class, residents read *Hope in the Unseen* in which Ron Suskind, a reporter from the *Wall Street Journal*, tells the story of a young African American man who went through the Washington, DC, public school system and eventually attended Brown University. The narrative demonstrates the complex challenges of low-income students of color who are often successful academically in their urban public school settings but severely underprepared for a rigorous college environment. In discussing the intersections of race, class, gender, language, sexuality, and ability, residents juxtapose their own experiences with those of the young man in the text. These preliminary conversations begin to shed light on the privilege that many residents bring to Newark and their relationships with urban youth.

The faculty and Newark community partners thought that having residents participate in several community-based internships would further the third space framework, provide valuable perspectives on Newark youth and highlight some strengths and needs of their communities. Building strong relationships with Newark youth would offer insights into the complexities of the students' identities and begins to illustrate the "funds of knowledge" of their families, homes, and communities (Gonzalez, Moll, & Amanti, 2005). Working with these organizations would help residents get to know Newark and begin to recognize its many community resources.

In addition, the community organizations could accommodate inquiry teaching and authentic learning without the constraints of a set curriculum, standards, and testing found in schools. Here residents could facilitate learning that was meaningful, engaging, and relevant to the Newark students. For example, one year, residents developed a zombie inquiry curriculum, which produced deep student engagement. While challenging, these experiences help residents see the power of relating curricula to students' lives. They can also to take risks, collaborate with one another, experience trial and error, and formulate beliefs about teaching and learning.

MENTORING NEWARK YOUTH

Besides their internships, residents mentor a Newark All Star youth who is interning in a corporate setting. A privately funded development program for poor, urban youth of color, Newark All Stars focuses on the social, cultural, and creative development of urban youth through performance. Project leaders believe that by focusing on community, performance, and creativity in and out of school, and bringing together corporate executives, artists, dancers, and others to dialogue and perform, urban youth can develop some of the tools they need to succeed in the real world. Their message to the youth is— "You don't just live in your socially over-determined, parochial neighborhood. You live in the world. And your participation in the new community can develop you to be a builder of the world, a more cosmopolitan citizen" (All Stars Project, 2007, 4).

While residents mentor their All Stars youths, in many ways the experience allows for "an exchange of insider information," as one resident put it. Residents guide the youth in navigating a professional corporate setting and the youth introduce residents to adolescent life in Newark. As part of their mentoring role, residents organized at least one social experience with their mentee and visited him or her at their assigned corporate internship site.

After six weeks of mentoring, residents write a case study about their mentee, reflecting on the implications of their shared experiences and on their emerging identity as an urban teacher. Besides producing a rounded portrait, they analyze and interpret their shared experiences, using evidence to support their developing understandings. The experience greatly influences residents' thinking about themselves as teachers. As one resident wrote:

> Through my interactions, I have gotten to know some of the realities that urban youth face regarding safety, mobility, and common differences in family structure. Regardless of these differences, I believe that all people, both adults and children, desire respect, autonomy, and acceptance. I learned that a lot of them are looking for connections which is particularly important in the urban environment. When the students got to know us, they were more than happy to work with us to do something or to help us. (Resident, 2013)

BECOMING SOCIAL JUSTICE TEACHERS: THE INQUIRY CYCLE EXPERIENCE

The summer experiences lay a solid foundation for the program's social justice paradigm which rests on from Freire's (1970) "problem posing pedagogy" and which integrates the research and practices of funds of knowledge (Gonzalez et al., 2005). According to this paradigm, students are considered constructors of knowledge, and teaching is built upon the experiences, language, and cultures of the students. But how would residents learn to enact this kind of teaching? How would they learn to design math and science curricula with a social justice orientation?

From the beginning, the program embraced inquiry as a way to examine the social and cultural norms that are constructed and re-constructed in schools (Short, Harste, & Burke, 1996). The fall semester is devoted to helping residents understand what socially just inquiry in math and science teaching entails and design units in keeping with this orientation. The spring semester is a time for constructing curricula that help high school students make sense of their worlds. This happens through a curricular structure called an inquiry cycle experience project (ICE).

Before residents create their own inquiry cycle, the faculty facilitate and model the experience by creating learning stations and an inquiry project around issues of race and class in schooling. A typical inquiry cycle begins with questioning, problem-posing, or a "wondering and wandering" phase to spark a question (Short et al., 1996). Then follows an investigation of the question or problem, a synthesis or creation based on the results of the investigation, sharing and discussing the synthesis, reflection on the process, and sometimes an action (Freire, 1970).

To launch this group inquiry, residents rotated through learning stations, examining texts, music, and videos related to the theme of social justice in schooling, taking notes, brainstorming questions, and writing reflections about their experiences in the learning stations. Residents were then asked to design and teach an ICE unit in their own discipline. The units were supposed to build on students' interests, revolve around authentic, open-ended questions, require students to gather various kinds of data, and conclude with a dissemination of findings. The residents taught these units to their students in the high school classrooms toward the end of the spring semester. They also presented their ICE projects, including a rationale, lesson plans, graphic organizers, student work examples, and learning reflections to the faculty, mentors, and their peers.

Unit topics included rates of asthma, the availability of organic food, the production and processing of garbage, the amount of electrical energy used. Students designed research projects to examine these issues, collecting data in the field and presenting their findings. For example, one group of high school students examined the access Newark families have to fresh organic produce. The following year, this resident, now new high school teacher, collaborated with a colleague from the program to plan, develop, and maintain an urban garden where students grew fresh fruits and vegetables. He reflected that when students have projects "that are their own," the quality of their work and the level of their motivation increases greatly. He also recognized how social justice teaching gives students the opportunity to "cultivate their own voices on issues that are relevant to them" (Taylor & Klein, 2015).

USING VIDEO WITH MENTOR TEACHERS

Constructing a third space partnership is often a fragile, even utopian enterprise. Long-standing, complex hierarchies stand in the way of such work. This was particular striking in working with the mentor teachers. As they embarked on the year-long residency, university faculty assumed that telling mentor teachers they were "co-teacher educators" would make that so. By the end of year one, however, it became clear that the traditional roles of classroom teacher as owner of "practical" knowledge and university professor as holder of "theoretical knowledge" had been recreated. University faculty designed and implemented the new curriculum while mentor teachers focused on classroom experiences. Figuring out how to disrupt this traditional dynamic became the goal of the next year's residency.

Helping mentors think aloud. One successful strategy involved finding ways for faculty and mentors to study their own teacher education practices together, including mentoring practices. This profoundly shifted the dynamic among the different participants (Taylor & Klein, 2015). Two faculty, a number of mentor teachers, and a doctoral student began meeting weekly to talk about the challenges of mentoring. During these conversations, a key mentoring challenge emerged—how to help mentors make transparent their interactive decision-making and problem solving. As one mentor put it, "I can't even verbalize sometimes why I've done something. It feels like it's natural. I think I've just been teaching for so long and I've had so many student teachers that, for me, it isn't difficult."

This propelled mentors and faculty to seek a way to articulate the often unnamed work of teaching. One idea involved the use of videos to help teachers "name" teaching decisions and reveal why they do what they do. Since the program aims to prepare inquiry-based math and science teachers, residents needed to learn to use teaching methods they may not have experienced as students. Having mentors articulate the thinking behind their use of inquiry methods was critical to that learning process (Taylor & Klein, 2015).

The protocol required mentors or residents to videotape themselves teaching and then choose a clip to share with each other. First mentors videotaped themselves and modeled the process for the residents, choosing a motif to focus the viewing. The video protocols also supported the integration of theory and practice. Videotapes of mentors' teaching provided opportunities for residents to "catch" and unpack the ways their mentors enacted theories which had been discussed in classes.

Mentors found they could also teach theory through conversations around videotapes. Often what seemed automatic and un-thought-out to residents was in fact deeply intentional on the part of the mentors. Mentors had theories and intentions that guided their classroom actions. When prompted to reveal why they did what they did, they could make connections among content, students, and pedagogy. Over and over residents were able to "see" examples of "engagement," "inquiry," and "student-centered teaching" in practice, ideas frequently discussed frequently in faculty-led courses. Some mentors used video-based discussions to model practices they wanted their resident learn. They could point to something in their video and say: "See, this is an example of where students get to ask questions and construct their own knowledge."

CONCLUSION: BUILDING SUSTAINABLE CHANGE

> The NMUTR supported my growth as a socially just teacher leader and it has allowed me the opportunity to help produce and develop outstanding teachers. . . . Of the six residents I have mentored in the program, five have been hired within the school and it has been nothing but exciting and rewarding to watch them grow as educators. Mentoring has forever changed my own philosophy of education to one that is centered on the necessary support and community based efforts required to educate our urban youth. In a small way I feel as though I am not teaching only my five classes of students, but through collaborative efforts and working, I am also reaching the students of my former residents and current peers. (Mentor teacher, 2013)

The program relied on three main strategies for promoting sustainable school change. First, the program counted on graduates to assume leadership roles in their schools by creating school communities that foster socially just inquiry-based curriculum. Second, the program built collaborative reciprocal relationships with mentors, supporting their growth as teacher leaders and their work as change agents. Third, working closely with principals and department chairs strengthened the likelihood that the vision of the "third space" residency as a vehicle for sustainable change in schools would be realized.

In developing the program, faculty leaders thought strategically about the boundaries of our spheres of influence. By working collaboratively with district administrators, school principals, and math and science department chairs at our partner high schools in Newark, they sought to foster a sense of agency among an intergenerational cadre of teacher leaders, both mentors and residents. They assumed that leadership for change would involve a "mutual dependency" or "a joint enterprise involving leaders and teachers in a reciprocal activity of realising the organisation's core objectives" (Haugh, Norenes, & Vedoy, 2014, 358). They hoped that faculty would also support and sustain this change through their conversations with mentors about articulating their practice.

At East Side High School, for example, the principal saw the residency as an opportunity to make change from within the building. He knew from the literature on leadership and school change that he played a key role as principal in creating the conditions necessary for teacher leaders to flourish (Taylor, Goeke, Klein, Onore, & Geist, 2011) and he worked with his department chairs to provide strategic opportunities for mentor teachers and residents to initiate new programs, design curriculum, and innovate teaching.

The science and math department chairs also saw the residency as a vehicle to ignite pedagogical change among the mentors and other teachers, mainly shifting from traditional teaching methods to a focus on inquiry-based learning (Taylor & Otinsky, 2007). On several occasions, teachers who were not participating directly in the residency took advantage of the presence of the NMUTR faculty and their focus on inquiry to improve their own teaching practices and increase their students' engagement and ultimately their achievement.

For instance, one mentor and resident invited another mathematics teacher to attend their Honors Pre-Calculus class on a daily basis. This invitation gave the other teacher an opportunity to observe and participate in the kinds of inquiry-based practices encouraged by the NMUTR. He then used these strategies in his own teaching, which led to his being rated as a "highly effective teacher."

The following year, his first year teaching Advanced Placement Calculus, this teacher's students received scores of 3s, 4s, and a 5, scores that in most cases give the students college credit. The same teacher coached two teams who won first place in both the Calculus and Pre-Calculus competitions of the Newark Math Olympics. He attributes these achievements to his learning experiences with the mentor and her resident. Rather than receiving a formal directive from the principal or department chair to change his pedagogy, the teacher was influenced by the mentor and her resident.

A "third space" partnership needs constant attention through honest dialogue and reflection in order to achieve its goal of promoting socially just, sustainable changes in schools. It also underscores the value of multiple perspectives and the need for flexible expectations and responsibilities. Such a multidimensional, third space framework allows a variety of stakeholders with unique strengths, experiences, and positions of power to work collectively toward the goal of school change. The model meets people where they are and allows them to position themselves as agents of change and to grow in ways that align with social justice teaching and inquiry-based pedagogy.

REFERENCES

All Stars Project, Inc. (2007). *Helping youth to grow.* New York.

Bhabha, H. K. (1994). *The location of culture.* London: Routledge.

Dewey, J. (1916). *Democracy and education: An introduction to the philosophy of education.* New York: Free Press.

Freire, P. (1970). *Pedagogy of the oppressed.* New York: Seabury Press.

Gonzalez, N., Moll, L., & Amanti, C. (2005). Introduction: Theorizing practice. In N. Gonzalez, L. C. Moll, & C. Amanti (Eds.), *Funds of knowledge: Theorizing practices in households, communities, and classrooms* (pp. 1–24). New York: Routledge.

Haugh, T. E., Norenes, S. O., & Vedoy, G. (2014). School leadership and educational change: Tools and practices in shared school leadership development. *Journal of Education Change, 15,* 357–376.

Papay, J. P., West, M. R., Fullerton, J. B., & Kane, T. J. (2012). Does an urban teacher residency increase student achievement? Early evidence from Boston. *Educational Evaluation and Policy Analysis, 34*(4), 413–434.

Pilburn, M., Sawada, D., Falconer, K., Turley, J., Benford, R., & Bloom, I. (2000). *Reformed Teaching Observation Protocol (RTOP).* Tempe, AZ: Arizona Collaborative for Excellence in the Preparation of Teachers.

Short, K. G., Harste, J. C., & C. Burke. (Eds.). (1996). *Creating classrooms for authors and inquirers.* Portsmouth, NH: Heinemann.

Solomon J. (2009). The Boston teacher residency: District-based teacher education. *Journal of Teacher Education, 60*(5), 478–488.

Suskind, R. (1999). *A hope in the unseen.* New York: Broadway Books.

Taylor, M., Goeke, J., Klein, E. J., Onore, C. & Geist, K. (2011). Changing leadership: Teachers lead the way for schools that learn. *Teaching and Teacher Education, 27,* 920–929.

Taylor, M., & Klein, E. J. (2015). *A year in the life of an urban teacher residency: Using inquiry to reinvent math and science education.* Rotterdam, the Netherlands: Sense.

Taylor, M. & Otinsky, G. (2007). Becoming whole language teachers and social justice agents: Pre service teachers inquire with sixth graders. *International Journal of Progressive Education, 3*(2), 59–71.

Chapter Nine

Teacher Education and Digital Learning

Reconstructing a Role for the University

Jae-Eun Joo and Bob Moon

In the last few decades, teacher education has come under considerable scrutiny. A major weakness is the separation of schools from universities. Digital learning not only offers new ways of improving teaching, it also provides an important means of bringing the world of schools and universities closer together. The increasingly social, networked dimension to new modes of communication is already influencing teacher education and other areas of higher education.

This chapter opens up questions about how digital networks and learning might be appropriated to the task of educating teachers. The chapter has three parts. The first examines challenges facing teacher education as the context in which digital learning merits consideration. The second looks at how digital learning might reconfigure the space and relationship between schools and universities and what newly emerging digital applications might be relevant to the education of teachers. The third makes the case for a more systematic integration of digital learning into the design of teacher education.

CHALLENGES FOR TEACHER EDUCATION

Since the 1990s, teacher education in the United States, Europe, and Australia has been challenged by those who believe that teacher education lacks relevance, is insufficiently practical, and is too concerned with abstract theorizing (Moon, 2016). Such criticism has led to the creation of new routes into teaching which bypass universities. A recent study of global models of teacher preparation (Moon, 2016) shows that such critiques exist all over the world.

Most of the highly politicized discussion about improving teacher education focuses on pre-service preparation with in-service teacher professional development receiving little political attention. New models of university-led teacher education that make full use of the potential of new communications technology and digital learning have the potential to address these specific issues and contribute to the improvement of teacher education at all levels.

RECONCEPTUALIZING THE SPACE BETWEEN SCHOOLS AND UNIVERSITIES

The distance between schools and universities in the education of teachers is a result of logistics and culture. Schools are rarely close to universities, and university faculty have become accustomed to working within the university. The supervision of pre-service student teachers is a low-status academic task, often delegated to graduate students or seconded teachers. University-led in-service professional development is rarely school based. Unless universities seize the opportunity to engage with hybrid models of teacher education, university-led teacher education is likely to disappear (Zeichner, 2016).

The Potential of Digital Technologies to Link Universities and Schools

The digital age offers very significant opportunities for overcoming the separation between schools and universities. Productive modifications in cultural relationships would follow the initiation of environments and program architecture. This can be seen in numerous examples where digital opportunities are being grasped at the institutional level.

The Rotterdam School of Education has been developing an Educational Plaza which forms a virtual space in which students and faculty maintain continuous contact. Allied to this is a Learning Network Education which operates as a communication platform between schools and the university (Brummelhuis, Wigngaars, Swager, & Gouzen, 2010). The Harvard Graduate School of Education now offers school-based and school-focused continuing professional development across a range of topics, using social media to ensure engagement with faculty and staff and peer-to-peer interaction.

Groups of teachers join collaborative improvement programs and take courses using such resources as videos, just-in-time guidance, adaptable presentation slides, templates for documenting group progress, and online access to others engaged in similar improvement programs. Besides having access to these resources, the teaching staff provides timetabled, online support sessions for each registered group (www.gse.harvard.edu).

OERs and MOOCs: New Ways to Network Teacher Education

In some parts of the world, collaborative inter-institutional forums are being set up. The Teacher Education in Sub-Saharan Africa (TESSA) program involves universities from ten countries, collaborating through a common portal (www.tessafrica.net) to provide high-quality, multilingual teaching resources and social forums to significantly improve the quality of school-based teacher education. Independent evaluations available on the TESSA website confirm their quality. TESSA is one of the first Open Educational Resources (OERs) working at scale in teacher education. In 2016, there were over 300,000 teachers, coordinated by university departments across the continent.

The impact of OERs is growing in higher education. The impetus came from a project at the Massachusetts Institute of Technology (MIT) to make all course resources freely available through an OpenCourseWare project (www.ocw.mit.edu). Started in 2002, the project now covers more than 2,000 MIT courses. These resources can be used as they are or adapted to a particular context. The Creative Commons licensing system, which now supports OER development, allows the originators of OERs to hold some control over future use. Some licenses permit completely open use while others stipulate that the OERs must not be used for commercial purposes.

OERs are significantly expanding the range of digital resources on which teacher education program can draw, and many new OER programs are being developed (Hewlett Foundation, 2013). The TESSA program in Africa has been followed by a multi-million-dollar initiative in India funded by the UK's Department for International Development (DFID). TESS India (www.tess.india.edu.in) has created teacher development units as well as leadership units for teachers and school leaders to use in pre-service and professional development settings. The resources are adapted to the different regional settings in which TESS India operates.

The goals of TESS India could be applied to many forms of teacher education across the globe, as the first two objectives illustrate:

- To make activity-based OERs available to teachers in various formats (print, online, CD/DVD, SD cards for mobile phones) to promote school-based practice for their own professional development;
- To engage teacher educators in learner-centered and activity-based pedagogical approaches via OERs and orientation programs.

One important purpose of OERs is to provide a knowledge base for the professional development process. The teacher educator, through face-to-face contact and/or online social interaction, can then give more time to the implementation and improvement processes. This principle undergirds the TESSA approach and is at the heart of the movement initiated by MIT.

Linked to the OER movement is the increasing interest in Massive Open Online Courses (MOOCs). These are usually short courses using online resources and communication to meet as wide an audience as possible. Stanford University in the United States was early into MOOCs. In 2011, it offered a course on Artificial Intelligence that reached 160,000 teachers. A number of consortia, among them Future Learn (www.futurelearn.com), have been established to exploit the potential of MOOCs.

The TESS India program uses units developed to create MOOCs. France has created an Open Classrooms site (www.openclassrooms.com) to make MOOCs (mostly in French but increasingly other languages) accessible to all. The Open Classrooms slogan is *Des Professeurs brilliant et des élèves géniaux* (Bright teachers, great students).

MOOCs have generated considerable controversy. Detractors question quality and completion rates. Supporters point to accessibility and the sheer richness of resources available. MOOCs now come in many formats, from those with a fairly traditional teaching model to new forms of digital capabilities. This argument will be ongoing as higher education and professional education begin to integrate digital modes of working into mainstream practice.

The evolution of OERs and MOOCs offers many important opportunities for teacher educators. Teacher education, particularly post pre-service, operates at large scale in most education systems. A technology designed for working at scale offers the potential to reach out to teachers in ways previously not possible.

In addition, many online digital teacher professional development sites are emerging, sometimes involving university staff. TeachMeet in the UK (teachmeet.pbworks.com) has grown from its small beginnings in Scotland to activities that spread across most parts of the UK. TeachMeet begins online but then provides well-attended opportunities for teachers to meet and exchange ideas. For example, one TeachMeet session held at Cheney School, Oxford, in December 2014 invited teachers to focus on classroom activities and strategies across a range of subjects. The brief for the meeting read:

> This is a chance to learn something new, be amazed, amused and enthused. This is an informal gathering of those curious about teaching and learning. Anyone can share great ideas they've trialed in their classrooms, ask important questions or simply sign up to take part in conversations about learning.

TeachMeet is about engaging and inspiring and making connections with other educators.

Over 100 teachers participated in this event. The approach is less formal than traditional continuing professional development. Looking at the briefs for a number of TeachMeet events, there is an edge of irreverence, which explains some of the appeal. TeachMeet events usually have input from well-known educationalists, many of whom work in universities. EdCamps in the United States represents a similar development.

Integrating Digital Technologies into Practice

The new modes of digital learning go beyond the mere provision of resources. The Harvard and Rotterdam initiatives include extensive online support. Support can also allow collaborative forms of development through social media that depend on varying degrees of formality or structure. However, these new models and approaches are still at an early stage of development. Building a stronger evidence base for what works for different teachers in varying contexts is clearly a necessity.

At present, many programs work outside the main structures of university-based teacher education. Perhaps the growing scale of online activity presages a change in organizational structures. How long will this take? If the university is to retain and develop its place in teacher education, the creation of new networks and relationships that utilize digital technologies to the full must become a much higher priority.

Of course, there is always resistance to innovative and potentially disruptive technologies. But challenge is integral to establishing successful new structures and systems. The sometimes fraught discussions around OERs, MOOCs, and digital learning generally suggest that we are in an important transition phase. Many commentators and analysts have examined the polarization of positions and the caricaturing of advocates and resisters (Davidson, 2013; Petriglieri, 2013).

Digital learning will reshape but not replace conventional modes of provision. It also opens up new opportunities to address the lack of involvement between teachers in schools and universities. Teachers rarely have the chance to engage with specialists in the age group and subjects for which they are responsible. This could change if new ideas about networks were developed.

The Future World of Digital Technologies Within the University

A range of innovations, many close to widespread adoption, could have great significance for teacher education. Futures spotting can quickly look outdated, but here are some examples which illustrate the relevance of digital technologies to teacher education. The examples are drawn from the New

Media Consortium Horizon Report on Higher Education produced as part of the EDUCAUSE program in 2015 (Johnson, Adams Becker, Estrada, & Freeman, 2015).

The report lists six technologies with the potential to foster real change in education: bring your own device (BYOD), flipped classrooms, maker-spaces, wearable technologies, adaptive learning technologies, and the Internet of things.

These technologies can support the development of progressive technologies and learning strategies, the organization of teachers' work, and the arrangement and delivery of content. Each has implications across higher education and each may help in linking universities, students, mentor teachers, and schools.

BYOD and flipped classrooms are now at the near-adoption phase. BYOD refers to the practice of people bringing their own laptops, tablet, or smart phone and connecting to the different institutional networks they use. BYOD is now spreading to higher education.

For instance, proponents at Griffith University in Australia cite mobile-device use as a way for students to learn material more effectively. A Bradford Network Study has shown that 85% of responding institutions allow faculty to use their own devices on campus and 52% said that such devices were being integrated into classroom teaching. Kings College London has implemented a private cloud platform that allows students and faculty from 150 countries to use their own devices to access a virtual desktop (www.go.nmc.org/kin).

The University of Pittsburgh is constructing three innovative classrooms to serve as models for future learning spaces. These classrooms feature technologies that enable students and instructors to use their own mobile devices to wirelessly and securely share documents, collaborate on projects, and display content in the rooms (www.go.nmc.org.scal).

One obstacle to taking up online and digital technologies has been the cost and upkeep of equipment. This is now disappearing as devices such as tablets and increasingly sophisticated mobile telephones become a part of everyone's everyday toolkit. This is true of poorer parts of the world as well, given the astonishing growth in mobile telephony. Teacher education planning and policy could exploit these new modes of accessibility.

The flipped classroom is another application close to adoption. With the goal of shifting ownership of learning from the teacher to the student, the flipped classroom uses technologies (including BYOD) to make ideas about blended and inquiry-based learning easier to implement. The Flipped Classroom Network is working to define and differentiate flipped learning approaches by analyzing research studies, archived webinars, examples of video usage, and much more.

Boston University has developed and begun implementing a new flipped course model that depends on building local, collaborative learning communities of faculty and graduate and undergraduate students (www.go.nmc.org/ bucon). There is considerable potential for linking teachers and pedagogic and academic specialists through the flipped classroom model.

Marketspaces and wearable technologies, the third and fourth technologies, have an adoption timeline of two to three years from 2016. In *Makerspaces*, the worlds of design and engineering begin to have significant influence over the educational environment. Proponents of makerspaces for education highlight the benefits of engaging learners in creative, higher-order problem solving through hands-on design, construction, and iteration. New technologies such as 3D printers and 3D modeling web-based applications become part of the tool set for those working in the makerspaces.

In a sense, marketspaces are a more open-ended flipped classroom, with the future bringing science teachers in a school district collaborating with university specialists in rethinking part of a curriculum structure. Agency by Design, a research initiative at the Harvard Graduate School of Education's Project Zero, seeks to investigate how a maker-centered approach to learning can help develop a students' sense of competency or agency (www.go.nmc.org.agan).

Within two to three years, it should be possible to incorporate wearable technology into our teaching and learning strategies. Google Glass enables users to see information about their surroundings, and Open Colleges, Australia's interactive infographic, is exploring the potential of Google Glass in education for activities such as documenting learning and remote teaching and instruction (www.go.nmc.org/glassmight).

The infrequent and clumsy tradition of lesson observations in teacher education could be conceived in quite different terms as this technology becomes more common. We now have the possibility of a more public, ongoing sharing of practice along with stronger and deeper discourse. This in itself will not create improved teaching or more trusting relationships between the observed and the observer. New protocols about access will need to be developed and observations prepared for and incorporated into the planning of new modes of provision.

A four- to five-year timeframe is envisaged for widespread adoption of the final two technologies—adaptive learning technologies and the Internet of things. *Adaptive learning technologies* refer to software and online platforms that adjust to individual students' needs as they learn. Adaptive learning is a sophisticated, data-driven, and in some cases non-linear approach to instruction and remediation. It allows for the adjustment of instruction to a learner's interactions and demonstrated performance level and the anticipation of needed content and resources to enable progress in learning (see http:/ /educationgrowthadvisors.com/gatesfoundation).

There are two levels to adaptive learning technologies. The first platform reacts to individual user data and adapts instructional media accordingly, while the second leverages aggregate data across a large sample of learners for insights into the design and adaptation of curricula. These sophisticated technologies might have important implications for how we come to understand and judge quality and performance in the classroom. They open up some fascinating prospects for university-school research programs.

For example, if teachers had more detailed profiles of individual or group learning, how could this information be pedagogically deployed? Brandman University in California, working with Flat World Education, has developed an online, competency-based business administration degree using deep adaptive learning technologies (go.nmc.org/flatm). A recent Gallup and Inside Higher Ed survey revealed that two out of three college and university presidents believe that adaptive technologies would positively impact higher education (Zimmer, 2014).

Finally, there is the *Internet of things*, a network of connected objects that link the physical world with the world of information through the web. Learners carrying such devices can benefit from a host of inter-disciplinary information. One example is a learner exploring a city, calling on architectural, political, or biological lenses to understand what they see. The teacher in the classroom should be able to use the same technology, drawing on ready-for-purpose resources for individual or collective use.

Cisco is currently teamed up with Melbourne's Swinburne University of Technology to collaborate on new research initiatives in this area (www.go.nmc.org/everything). Perhaps most significantly, the Internet of things offers the possibility of interactively using large data sets about the success of past pedagogic practices in terms of student achievement to inform future practice at the level of the individual class and student.

Painting such future scenarios can quickly look dated, not the least because the six overlapping technologies will be disrupted by interaction with each other and through the arrival of even newer applications. The point is rather simple—the technologies now exist to fuse the worlds of university, teacher educator, teachers, and schools in ways hitherto impossible. Exploiting them to enhance the value of teacher education seems essential.

SYSTEMIC USE OF DIGITAL LEARNING TO LINK SCHOOLS AND UNIVERSITIES

The need to reconstruct and reconfigure the relationship between universities and schools in teacher education is clear. A new architecture should take advantage of digital collaboration that can enrich, rather than replace, the best practices of teacher education. Clearly some are cautious about incorporating digital learning into their work; however, the best forms of teacher education mirror and extend good school-teaching practice.

The use of digital technologies in schools is rapidly evolving, and teacher education can also embrace more integrated forms of practice. Adapting the curriculum and organization of teacher education to these new spatial relationships will mean cultural shifts in the way teachers and teacher educators work. This is not necessarily a radical shift in perspective.

Discussions about new technologies proceed alongside long-standing debates about the relationship of theory to practice and the place of practice in the curriculum of teacher education. Technology does not render these debates obsolete. Rather it provides the means for wider and different responses than were previously possible. More networked modes of working, the capacity to blend face to face and other forms of communication in more networked and perhaps less hierarchical structures, offers great potential for bringing the worlds of schools and universities closer together.

This is not the first time that rapid changes in forms of communication have had the potential to significantly influence our ambitions for educational and social progress. The printing press, the telegraph, the telephone all changed conceptions of the world. The end of the nineteenth century was a time of rapid change as the world was united through a net of steel, telegraph wires, and ideologies of progress.

Perhaps more significant, for the first time in history, growing numbers of people saw themselves as inhabiting a space beyond the here and now (Erlmann, 1999). New forms of socio-spatial imagination inscribed themselves in the very syntax of language, the "intersections of absence and presence" as Giddens (1991) has called them. Into the new spaces created by rapid changes of technology came "new cultural intermediaries" and new roles for intellectuals (Bourdieu, 2005).

Such rapid change is also characteristic of the newly emergent digital technologies available today. Teacher educators, like others within the university, can exploit these technologies, drawing on interesting new ideas about reconstructing ideas and practices. For example, there has been a resurgence of interest in the ways in which contemporary ideas about design can be applied to the reconstruction of social policies and practices. Mathew Taylor (2014) contrasts policy makers who try to get things right and often suffer the consequences of failure with the rest of us with designers who use experimental methods, trying things out and learning from failure. This requires the ability to look not just at what people say, but how they actually live and use products and services.

The prevailing policy orthodoxy relies on a simplistic view of human motivation, while designers engage product and service users in the very process of design, deriving inspiration from the way people adapt existing ideas and services (Joo & Moon, 2015; Taylor, 2014). Such thinking should inform the reconstruction of the space between teacher educators and the world of schools.

The university could become the hub for networks in which teacher educators and academic specialists provide intellectual support and leadership to teachers. Universities have the creative and technical capacity to manage a system made up of clusters of schools through which teachers gain access to network opportunities and resources.

These networks and sites will almost certainly engage in real-time interaction, but the processes that bind their activities are likely to include an increasingly digital element. Practice, as in fields such as medicine or law, will become the core of the curriculum but informed in a much more interactive way by knowledge, ideas, and experience from elsewhere. Such networks would allow teacher educators to maintain contact with teachers across career stages and to act as intermediaries between teachers and the academic resources of the university.

Take the teaching of secondary science. In many pre-service programs, the trainee science teacher has strong links with a teacher educator specializing in science. These one-on-one relationships can be very powerful and effective. Would it not be even more significant if academic scientists from across the university could be part of the network process that begins in pre-service and carries on to professional development programs? There may be face-to-face elements to this, but the processes that tie the network together would be digital. The teacher of young children might have a similar opportunity by bringing together specialists in child development and learning with teacher educators working in the area.

Such networks could develop in many different ways, depending on important logistical and substantial pedagogic matters. New systems of governance will be needed along with reformed funding structures. Some universities today are trying to bolt on digital learning without seriously reviewing the implications for the system as a whole. There is also the challenge of ensuring that faculty, staff, and teachers in schools have the skills, knowledge, and understanding to cooperate effectively within new forms of program design. This will need to be built into the planning and design process.

The central argument of this chapter is that we need to move beyond an incremental approach to digital learning. There are many piecemeal explorations of digital affordances but the merging of these into a reformed and realigned model of teacher development at a systemic level is still missing. Creatively meeting this challenge will be central to securing and expanding the role of universities in teacher education.

REFERENCES

Bourdieu, P. (2005). *The social structure of the economy*. London: Polity Press.

Brummelhuis, A., Wigngaars, G., Swager, P., & Gouzen, B. (2010). *ICT in initial teacher training.* Paris: OECD.

Davidson, C. (2013). *Stop polarising the MOOCs debate.* Bill and Melinda Gates Foundation. Retrieved from http://www.impatientoptimists.org/Posts/2013/02/Stop-Polarising-the-MOOCs-Debate.

Erlmann, V. (1999). *Music, modernity and the global imagination.* Oxford: Oxford University Press.

Giddens, A. (1991). *Modernity and self-identity: Self and society in the late modern age.* Cambridge, UK: Cambridge University Press.

Hewlett Foundation. (2013). *Open educational resources: Breaking the lockbox on education.* Menlo Park, CA: Hewlett Foundation.

Johnson, L., Adams Becker, S., Estrada, V., & Freeman, A. (2015). *NMC Horizon Report: 2015 higher education edition.* Austin, TX: The New Media Consortium.

Joo, J., & Moon, B. (2015). Rethinking the design approach to digitally enhanced curriculum development. *The Curriculum Journal, 26*(2), 335–339.

Moon, B. (Ed.). (2016). *Do universities have a role in the education and training of teachers? An international analysis of policy and practice.* Cambridge UK: Cambridge University Press.

Pentriglieri, G. (2013). Let them eat MOOCs. *Harvard Business Review*, October 9.

Taylor, M. (2014). The policy presumption. *Journal of the Royal Society of Arts, 4*, 10–15.

Zeichner, K. (2016). The changing role of universities in US teacher education. In B. Moon (Ed.), *Do universities have a role in the education and training of teachers? An international analysis of policy and practice.* Cambridge UK: Cambridge University Press.

Zimmer, T. (2014). Rethinking higher education: A case for adaptive learning. *Forbes*, October 22.

Chapter Ten

Creating an Online Teacher Preparation Program

Melora Sundt, Margo Pensavalle, and Karen Gallagher

This chapter describes how the University of Southern California (USC), one of the largest, private universities in the United States, designed, developed, and delivered the first online teacher preparation program of its kind. Drawing on seven years of experience, the authors discuss key decisions, missteps, impact data, and lessons learned. The challenges of scaling up and managing clinical practice are also considered.

INSTITUTIONAL CONTEXT AND HISTORY

Three significant events prompted USC to launch an online MAT program: a new provost, a re-examination of our vision, and a fortuitous meeting with an entrepreneur. In 2005, a new provost mandated that all schools would offer at least one online program. He further stipulated that online programs would use the same admissions criteria and charge the same tuition as on-campus programs and be limited to master's degree and professional doctorates.

The mission of USC's Rossier School of Education is to improve learning in urban environments locally, nationally, and globally. Our strategic plan presents a vision deeply committed to equity, where every student, regardless of personal circumstance, can learn and succeed. This mission and vision and the new provost's mandate ignited an interest in finding ways to increase the impact of the Master of Arts in Teaching (MAT) program. But how?

In 2008, a solution emerged. John Katzman created an endowed chair in Educational Entrepreneurship, Technology and Innovation at the Rossier School. As the founder of Princeton Review, John had developed a keen interest in K-12 education. When Princeton Review went public, John created a new educational technology company called 2Tor and challenged the education faculty to think about how to prepare highly qualified teachers by partnering with 2Tor in designing an online MAT program.

DESIGNING THE PROGRAM

Some administrators and faculty were skeptical about the possibility of delivering a quality program online, especially across a wide geographical range and with a serious clinical component. How could hiring qualified faculty keep pace with the increasing size of the program? How could faculty ensure coherent learning experiences, meaningful assessments, and consistent outcomes on a large scale? How could the teaching reflect a shared ideological framework?

The design team included the associate dean for academic programs, the director of teacher education, a faculty member, and a former associate superintendent working for 2Tor as chief academic officer. The team's charge was unprecedented: design the best teacher preparation program imaginable, based on research and the values of the school, and deliver it online.

Conceptual Framework

After numerous discussions, the design team identified the following core assumptions:

a. *The program should disrupt deficit thinking.* Pre-service teachers often come to our program with deficit notions about how learning occurs and who learners are. The program emphasizes the capacities of all learners and purposeful questioning as a form of disruptive, focused inquiry.
b. *Context and place influence teaching and learning outcomes.* Effective teachers understand the relationship between a school and its community, a classroom and its school, and a child and his/her school and community. Effective teaching adapts to the place, incorporating meaning from community experiences, values, and traditions.
c. *Understanding learning is central to effective teaching.* Teachers need more than formulaic methods. They need to understand the many ways students learn.

These assumptions respond to problems of practice in teacher education and learning to teach, for example, a deficit view of poor children and their communities, a lack of awareness about the relationship between structural oppression and learning outcomes, and a technical view of teaching.

The program was designed around seven substantive domains—advocacy, assessment, critical reflection and inquiry, curriculum, discourse and critical thinking, environment, and pedagogy. These domains framed the knowledge and skills candidates need to develop, drove performance goals and assessments, and informed course content.

Program Structure and Sequence

The program is organized around a developmental learning continuum consisting of two twelve-week sessions (Terms 1 and 2) and two ten-week sessions (Terms 3 and 4). In Term 1, candidates explore their identity as teachers, identify their strengths and biases, especially around the social context of schooling, and study learning theory. In Term 2, candidates integrate knowledge from Term 1 with knowledge of content and pedagogy. In Term 3, candidates gradually assume classroom responsibilities and start applying what they have been learning. Term 4 focuses on problem solving in the context of practice as candidates teach on a daily basis while continuing their instructional methods coursework.

The online curriculum was adapted to serve the on-ground program. As a result, syllabi and expectations for the two programs are identical. The same professors teach in both formats and the courses cover the same content and require the same amount of face-to-face class time. Both formats lead to the same degree, apply the same admissions standards, meet the same program and state credential requirements, charge the same tuition. Students from both formats are eligible for university services, academic support, and financial aid. All candidates do their guided practice in the communities where they live.

Most unusual, the online program is synchronous, not self-directed and self-scheduled as most online programs are. Students attend classes at a specific time with the same group of peers and the same professor. The online program has four cohort starts per year compared with one start for the on-ground program, and the online program is five-times larger than the on-ground MAT. These differences pose operational challenges.

Guided Practice

Guided practice, formerly called student teaching, is a staple in teacher preparation and a challenge for online learning. Traditionally, student teachers plan and teach lessons and cooperating teachers give feedback related to what went well and what could be improved. In the online MAT, we envisioned a different model. Candidates would send videotapes of their planning, teaching, and reflection to university faculty called "guiding instructors," who would review lesson plans and give feedback in a weekly Guided Practice seminar for groups of eight candidates.

After seven years, implementing this new model on a consistent basis still poses challenges. It requires classroom teachers and university professors to work in new ways. It requires considerable communication and follow-up and swift problem solving when issues arise. It also depends on candidates who can gradually build the necessary professional skills.

Students

The faculty's highest priority was that the program have intellectual and professional rigor. Admissions requirements align with the university's graduate admissions threshold, including a 3.0 GPA. Instead of GRE scores, applicants submit responses to essay questions. All secondary content candidates must complete twelve university level units in the content they plan to teach; multiple subject candidates must complete three university level units each in mathematics, English-language arts, science, and a social science. All candidates must pass a subject matter verification test before they begin all-day directed teaching.

Many candidates are second-language learners, the first in their families to graduate with a BA or BS degree, and committed to righting the wrongs of their own learning experiences. They enter the program with strong content knowledge and varying academic skill. Various support programs help strengthen students' writing ability and frequent, faculty-led webinars address a variety of teaching, learning, and professional topics.

The MAT online population is older than the students in the on-ground program, and often teaching is not their first career. Online candidates are twice as likely to do the program part-time, taking two years, rather than one to complete it. They also are more likely to work part-time and sometimes full-time until they reach Guided Practice in Term 3.

Online students currently live in forty-six states and twenty-three countries. Many candidates in other countries teach in international schools. Half come from California. They tend to be students from public university undergraduate programs, but also include graduates from top private schools.

Working with Partners

Building the program was both challenging and inspiring. Besides writing syllabi, course narratives were created to provide continuity. All courses use video, audio, and hands-on resources to scaffold learning assignments, class-time activities, and assessments. These had to be imagined, produced, edited, and placed onto the learning platform, with consistency and coherence across all course sections and program courses.

Most faculty had not taught online before, and few knew how to use the requisite tools. With increased enrollments, faculty loads increased exponentially. The 2U design team attended all design meetings which were creative times for faculty, and they offered guidance in course development.

The first cohort of students began the program in June 2009, just twelve months after the first design meetings. Support from senior administrators, faculty commitment, and assistance from partners enabled the rapid rollout of the program.

Staffing and Running the Program

The synchronous online program requires more and different staffing. To provide leadership in course development and implementation, the position of course coordinator was created. Course coordinators oversaw the writing and development of courses with help from 2U technology designers. When USC was 2U's only client, that support was plentiful.

Course coordinators are responsible for one or two courses with multiple sections. They recruit part-time faculty, convene weekly or bi-weekly course faculty meetings, oversee course implementation, and support faculty in course-related problems. For some, this responsibility counts toward a service load; others receive a stipend.

A second group, the MAT governance committee, makes all content and curriculum recommendations to the dean and associate dean. Day-to-day program administration is the responsibility of the director of the MAT program. The first director had a business background, and she worked with senior leadership on budget and personnel recommendations, served as liaison with services in the School of Education and worked with 2U to maintain financial and resource agreements.

Program Results

In the fall of 2015, 675 candidates were enrolled in the MAT with credential (68%), MAT degree only (9%), TESOL (17%), and Masters in Education (5%). Since the program's start, 2,600 candidates have completed these programs. While many factors affect online education retention rates (Hart, 2012), our candidates average 60%–70% on-time program completion.

In the fall of 2013, 87% of our graduates were employed in education, half in California. California, Florida, Georgia, and Texas were the top national employers. Korea, China, and Japan were the top international employers. Between 2011 and 2014, our graduates were employed on average in

295 schools, thirty-five states, and eighteen countries (Dean's Report, February 2015).

An external evaluation in the fourth year of the program reported that

- 74% of respondents were employed in formal and informal educational settings;
- 68% reported feeling "prepared" or "very prepared" to teach all students on the first day;
- 83% reported feeling capable of building strong relationships with students;
- 87.6% reported feeling able to maintain high academic expectations for their students.

Other external evaluations revealed that most graduates (89%) were teaching students from diverse backgrounds, including students with limited English proficiency (75%), students with IEPs (82%), struggling readers (92%), and students from low socio-economic backgrounds (85%).

Evaluating the work of graduates has proven more difficult due to the scale and geographic diversity of the program and California's decision not to use value added measurement of classroom teachers. Faculty participate in "Hub Trips" each year, using a consistent observation and interview protocol to collect data from program graduates, current candidates, guiding teachers, and school administrators to gauge the quality of candidates' and graduates' teaching.

In 2014–2015, faculty visited five national hubs and several local school sites. Anecdotal data from site administrators and guiding teachers suggest that they were very satisfied with student teachers' progress and level of content knowledge and thought the program was "very demanding." If their school had an opening, they would hire their student teachers.

At the same time, school administrators who did hire graduates found that their classroom management was weak at the beginning of the school year. Over time, however, teachers developed well-organized classrooms and "humanistic" approaches to management, knew their content, and created supportive environments for students.

In response to these data, a faculty committee worked on ways to increase candidates' knowledge of classroom environment, pedagogy, and curriculum and to help them translate this knowledge into classroom management practices. Courses have incorporated concepts of "restorative justice" and school-wide positive behavioral intervention and support.

Challenges and Lessons Learned

Mounting a large, synchronous, online teacher preparation program involved a steep learning curve. The biggest "lessons learned" related to the following areas: (a) working with the partner/vendor; (b) placements and oversite of student teaching; (c) learning to teach synchronously online; (d) staffing; (e) coordinating across the university; and (f) building the online community. Three themes—communication, use of data, and planning—cut across these major areas.

Working with the technology partner. A good partnership results from having shared goals as well as a clear and common contractual understanding by all parties. In launching a partnership with 2U, university faculty wondered how the culture and goals of a for-profit organization would mesh with those of a non-profit research university.

Delivering an outstanding online program was USC's overarching goal. There was some initial concern that the revenue-sharing nature of the contract might incentivize 2U to attempt to recruit unqualified candidates. Fortunately, the revenue sharing mechanism, combined with the division of responsibilities (see Table 10.1) generally supported the goal. 2U would realize revenue gains as the program grew, but the program would grow only if the program had its intended impact. Admitting unqualified candidates was in neither partner's interest.

This partnership was a first for USC and 2U, and both sides had much to learn. Two areas dominated the early work: boundaries and expectations. Because neither had built a partnership like this before, the negotiation of boundaries required extensive discussion and revisiting. Formal boundaries were initially spelled out in the contract. In practice, however, students reached out to the 2U admissions and student support staff with any manner

Table 10.1.   Division of Responsibilities Between USC Rossier and 2U

USC Rossier's Responsibilities	2U's Responsibilities
• Set admissions criteria • Make admissions decisions • Make scholarship decisions • Design all curricula • Teach all courses • Hire all faculty • Provide academic advising • Set placement criteria • Assist with school/district partnerships • Approve guiding teachers • Maintain accreditation	• Recruit new cohorts according to USC's criteria • Serve as first contact for program inquiries • Market program • Locate and coordinate placements • Pay for guiding teachers • Offer 24/7 tech and student support • On-board faculty and students onto platform • Build/maintain platform • Provide data about students/program • Establish state approval outside CA

of questions, unaware of the agreed-on division of labor. To address the problem, all 2U front-line staff received extensive training so they could answer student inquiries or direct them to appropriate USC resources.

The two partner organizations also had to mesh their different organizational cultures, particularly around expectations of turn-around time. 2U expected the university to respond much more quickly than was customary. This led the university to re-examine many of its processes, some of which were unnecessarily slow and burdensome. The preparation of admission files and admission application reviews received significant streamlining as a result.

A second area which required attention involved the learning management system. In building the system 2U focused on the needs of the students, and they did an excellent job. But they missed design elements needed by instructors. Besides course content, the platform had to hold grades and student work, needs not addressed by the first iteration. 2U adjusted the learning management system to make it more instructor-friendly.

A third area that required further negotiation was communication. Early on, it became clear that each organization needed one point person who met frequently to solve problems. The growth of 2U during the program design phase challenged this strategy. As 2U added new programs, they redirected experienced staff members with whom USC had built a solid relationship to staff these new programs. This resulted in communication delays and confusion.

Key components of a strong partnership emerged. They included (a) clear, commonly understood goals; (b) clearly defined responsibilities; (c) an agreement for resolving problems/disputes before they arise; (d) a point person for each side; (e) regular, frequent "check-ins"; and (f) trust building so the point people can be candid about program progress.

Oversight of Student Teaching

As in most teacher education programs, Guided Practice has many moving parts and requires constant attention. 2U is responsible for finding (and paying for) strong guiding teachers. The USC program requires guiding teachers to participate in an orientation before they receive their stipend. Besides holding Partnership Dinners, the program is working to solicit input guiding teachers and integrate them more fully into the program.

Besides the regular monitoring of candidates' work through video and classes, faculty annually visit candidates and graduates in several hub locations to observe and interview guiding teachers, candidates, graduates, and the administrators. These visits reach 5%–10% of the placement settings. Candidates evaluate their placement site and their guiding teacher at the end of each term. University instructors are supposed to communicate regularly with guiding teachers and district level partners.

A more complicated challenge concerns the credential which students earn. All candidates are prepared for a California credential, regardless of where they live. Out-of-state students can either seek qualification in their home state or pursue a California credential and then apply for reciprocity in their home state. But accommodating candidates who seek teaching credentials in other states remains a challenge, since state credentialing regulations frequently change as do state credentialing staff.

Staffing and Enrollment Projections

The rapid growth of the MAT program brought strikingly different responses from USC and 2U. The university could not staff the program on the basis of anticipated growth. They needed additional revenue. Because growth in enrollment came quickly, within a single fiscal year, there was insufficient time to anticipate needed staff. As a result, existing staff were taxed during the first period of expansion. By contrast, 2U had enough liquidity to increase their staff, which enabled them to absorb the growth in students.

Enrollment in the MAT proved volatile, with periods of rapid growth followed by decline. These surges made planning within a revenue-centered system challenging. University leaders worked with 2U to improve their ability to understand and predict admissions and retention numbers.

Increased student teaching hours led to a high drop in enrollment. Candidates with day jobs could not quit their job or adjust their work schedule. The financial impact was too great, so they dropped out. Once this problem was understood, the distribution of scholarships during the third and fourth terms of the program was modified to enable candidates to continue.

Coordinating with the University

The MAT was designed without regard for the university calendar. Courses were as long as they needed to be, rather than conforming to an artificial schedule. In the beginning, university offices such as financial aid, admissions, or the registrar's office were not consulted. Rather they were presented with the new program and were expected to adjust their infrastructures.

To their credit, colleagues across the university did their best to accommodate the new program. The initial steps in the university's admission process were revised, resulting in a faster process. The university created a new faculty role for full-time, off-site, non-tenure track faculty which enabled the hiring of exceptional faculty across multiple time zones. Less malleable was the financial aid process. Program leaders learned the hard way about the importance of including financial aid expertise in designing the program's calendar to ensure maximum eligibility for online students.

The Online Community

Based on available research, program leaders assumed that online students, like their on-campus counterparts would want (a) responsiveness, convenience, efficiency (Lowry, 2004; Shea, 2005); (b) ease of platform use (Samman, Omar, Balmasrour, & Alijani, 2013); and (c) a sense of community (Roper, 2007).

To help students feel part of the USC community, 2U's designers built several key features into the Learning Management System, including the ability to create student profiles and student groups, and student-initiated virtual meeting tools. These social networking features are absent in many other online platforms.

In the USC online community, students create their own profiles, create and join organizations, message each other, get to know one another and their faculty, and stay in touch, much like on Facebook. At first, faculty worried about losing the valued sense of community cultivated in the on-campus program. These tools and students' immediate use of them enabled them to know students better and enabled students to engage with one another outside of class to a greater extent than the on-campus cohorts. Still, there were lessons to be learned.

Student organizations and norms. Students quickly embraced the opportunity to create social groups through the Learning Management System. In some groups, however, students complained and shared misinformation about the program, assuming that someone from USC was paying attention. Students' frustration quickly went viral, spilling over into real Facebook postings. This highlighted the need for more intentional shepherding and development of online groups and greater responsiveness to students' questions and concerns.

2U created a staff position to facilitate the well-being of the online community, and Rossier charged its academic advisors to be present in this new online world. As the number of student groups increased, maintaining this level of facilitation was challenging. Violations of social norms in the co-curricular community and in the synchronous classes also increased. Some violations related to "presentation of self," including inappropriate dress; engaging in a simultaneous, unrelated activity; interacting with persons (or pets) who are not part of the class; leaving (or "freezing") the camera or behaving in an overtly inattentive manner. Others related to location, for instance, attending class in a place with loud background noise or visual distractions or a place like a library, where verbal participation is inhibited. Still others involved the manner of participation, such as students' inappropriate tone or language and failing to moderate their participation by not allowing others to speak or not listening.

Early norm-breaking led faculty to develop strategies for establishing and preserving appropriate expectations within the new virtual community. During orientation and the first meeting of each course, students learned about these expectations. Staff reminded students about the norms within social groups and students were invited to contribute to the creation and building of norms. A special forum for complaints, concerns, and feedback was created, and students were asked upon enrollment to sign a statement affirming their understanding of the community's norms and values.

CONCLUSION

Over 2,800 students have graduated from the online MAT program since the first cohort began in 2009. While program leaders were solving the intellectual, programmatic, and regulatory puzzles associated with offering a robust online program, the recession of 2007–2008 greatly affected state and national contexts of teacher education and subsequent school district budget cuts in all states. This often leads to layoffs for new teachers and deep uncertainty for more experienced teachers. Since program graduates often start as substitute teachers before getting more permanent positions, this affected employment opportunities.

Enrollments in the online MAT rose sharply in 2010–2011 and then dropped each year through 2013–2014. Enrollments have stabilized in the past year and are still five to six times larger than enrollments in the on-ground MAT.

Evidence from external evaluations shows that high-quality novice teachers can be prepared online. The pipeline for new teachers has expanded by offering synchronous classes, asynchronous access to materials, placements in schools close to where students live, and use of social media to form a strong professional community. The program has demonstrated that a non-profit university can partner with a for-profit company for services that benefit the university, the students, and the company.

But there are caveats. For this to work, university culture must value and support entrepreneurial ventures like the partnership with 2U. University staff responsible for registration, financial aid, and IT services must be problem solvers. Growth and decline contingencies must be built into contracts. It turns out that high-quality, online degree programs are as expensive as high-quality on-ground programs.

REFERENCES

Danis, C., & Lee, A. (2005). The evolution of norms in a newly forming group. *Human-Computer Interaction-INTERACT*, 522–535.

Dyson, E. (1999). *Release 2.0L: A design for living in the digital age.* New York: Broadway Books.

Floyd, D., & Casey-Powell, D. (2004). New roles for student support services in distance learning. *New Directions for Community Colleges, 128*, 55–64.

Hart, C. (2012). Factors associated with student persistence in an online program of study: A review of the literature. *Journal of Interactive Online Learning, 11*(1), 19–42.

Johnson, D. (2006). Signal-to-noise ratio. *Scholarpedia, 1* (12), 20–88.

Kretovics, M. (2003). The role of student affairs in distance education: Cyber-services or virtual communities. *Online Journal of Distance Learning Administration, 6* (3). Retrieved from http://www.westga.edu/~distance/ojdla/fall63/kretovics63.html.

Ludwig-Hardman, S., & Dunlap, J. (2003). Learner support services for online students: Scaffolding for success. *The International Review of Research in Open and Distance Learning, 4*(1). Retrieved from http://www.irrodl.org/index.php/irrodl/article/view/131/211.

Samman, E., Omar, A., Belmasrour, R., & Alijani, G. (2013). Strategic plan for enhancing online learning. *Information Systems Education Journal, 11*(2), 36–49.

Shea, P. (2005). Servicing students online: Enhancing their learning experience. *New Directions for Student Services, 112*, 15–24.

Venable, M. (2007). *Online career services: What do college students want and expect?* Paper presented at the 23rd Annual Conference on Distance Teaching and Learning, University of Wisconsin.

Wachter, R., Gupta, J., & Quaddus, M. (2000). It takes a village: Virtual communities in support of education. *International Journal of Information Management, 20*, 473–489.

Chapter Eleven

A Case of Inclusion in a Physical Education Teacher Preparation Program

Ronnie Lidor

In the last two decades, a number of educational, pedagogical, and techno-logical challenges have attracted worldwide attention by those involved in teacher preparation. These reflect various cultural, social, and political trends, including radical changes in technology consumption and use, striv-ing for social-political equality among minorities, and changes in the work/ leisure ratio in favor of increasing the leisure time for individuals and fami-lies (Clark, 2000).

Challenges in teacher preparation that have emerged from these trends include the technology challenge and the multi-culture challenge. Because we live in an era dominated by technology, teacher education students should be familiar with modern technological devices and recognize their practical implications. Unfortunately, despite breakthroughs in educational technolo-gy, many students are unaware of the potential contribution of technology to learning and teaching.

Living in a multicultural age poses other challenges for teacher education. Students from different cultures (e.g., natives and immigrants from other countries), as well as students from sub-cultures (religious and non-religious) may study together in the same program. Since they are required to spend time together inside and outside the classroom, one pedagogical-social chal-lenge is finding effective ways to encourage integration, increase mutual understanding, and build cultural-social bridges among these students.

Teacher education students also need to acquire pedagogical tools for teaching children from different cultures and sub-cultures. It is assumed that if pre-service students have task-relevant opportunities (e.g., in-class activities and out-of-class activities) that foster relationships and build trust, they may draw on these experiences when teaching children from different cultural backgrounds.

This chapter focuses on one additional challenge in teacher preparation that has emerged from current cultural-social trends—the inclusion challenge (see Forlin & Chambers, 2011; Oyler, 2011; Swanson Gehrke, & Cocchiarella, 2013). More specifically, it deals with the challenge of including disabled students in a program that prepares physical education (PE) teachers. The discussion draws on the experience of the Academic College at Wingate, which prepares PE teachers for kindergarten, elementary schools, and high schools and is considered the leading college in Israel in the field of exercise and sport sciences.

The chapter has three parts. Part one previews the dual system of teacher preparation in Israel—one at the universities and one in the academic colleges of education. Part two describes how the College at Wingate addresses the challenge of including disabled students into its program for physical education teachers. Part three offers some ideas about how to assess the effects of such efforts.

TEACHER EDUCATION IN ISRAEL: A DUAL SYSTEM OF PREPARATION

Israel has a dual system of teacher preparation, with programs offered in universities and academic colleges of education. In university-based programs, students study one or two major disciplines, completing their undergraduate disciplinary studies in three years and earning a Bachelor of Arts or a Bachelor of Science degree. Then they spend an additional year or two earning a teaching certificate which enables them to teach their discipline/s in high schools. There are no structural or substantive links between disciplinary studies and teacher preparation.

By contrast, teacher preparation programs at the academic colleges of education deliberately connect disciplinary and pedagogical studies. Students study their major discipline/s and simultaneously undertake pedagogical courses in each year of their four-year program. Upon completing the four-year program, students earn a Bachelor of Education and a teaching certificate which enables them to teach in elementary schools in Israel. In some fields and disciplines (e.g., arts, dance, PE), the teaching certificate enables students to teach in high schools as well.

The close connection between disciplinary studies and pedagogical studies at the colleges of education has a number of advantages, but one major limitation. By taking classes in their selected discipline/s and classes in pedagogy across the four-year program, students have a unique opportunity to integrate different types of knowledge. Students can apply concepts, ideas, and themes learned in their disciplinary classes in the pedagogical classes. They can also further develop some of the pedagogical ideas they study in their discipline-based courses. The assumption is that these connections strengthen teacher preparation.

Lecturers responsible for the two types of studies also have the opportunity to coordinate their classes. In addition, some classes use a co-teaching model. In these classes, students learn from a disciplinary expert as well as from an experienced teacher who provides real-world, instructional examples of how disciplinary knowledge can be effectively implemented in school classrooms.

This linking practice has one major limitation. Since the academic colleges of education are oriented around teaching and their main objective is to prepare students to be good and effective teachers, considerable emphasis is placed on pedagogical studies. Disciplinary studies are often relegated to a secondary role. The emphasis on increasing students' pedagogical knowledge rather than their disciplinary knowledge can lead to teachers who know how to teach but may lack fundamental knowledge about what to teach.

According to data reported by the Council for Higher Education in Israel, about 25,000 students were enrolled at the academic colleges of education in 2015 (Council for Higher Education, 2016). Among the 64,733 students who studied at the various universities in Israel in the same year, about 1,000 completed pedagogical/teaching studies in addition to their disciplinary studies, in order to be certified as teachers in high schools. An analysis of how many students obtained teaching certification in Israel during the last two decades reveals a similar pattern. The majority of students who complete pedagogy/teaching studies did so at the academic colleges of education, with only a small portion completing these studies at the universities.

THE INCLUSION ("RECEIVING THE OTHER") CHALLENGE

The increasing number of students with special needs who aspire to become elementary or high school teachers is one of the major challenges currently faced by the academic colleges of education in Israel. In addressing this challenge, the Academic College at Wingate modified the existing teacher preparation program in order to enable students with special needs to study at the same level as other students in the program.

Public Attention and Research Effort

Today greater public attention is being paid to the integration of individuals/ groups with special needs (see Jobling & Moni, 2004). The assumption is that mutual understanding among individuals/groups with various abilities, needs, and preferences can be increased if these individuals/groups come together in a given framework, including work, school, academic institutions, and leisure activities (see Lidor & Blumenstein, 2012). With the increased implementation of inclusive education, teacher educators have also been challenged to make programmatic changes in order to prepare students to educate diverse learners. It follows that if students with special needs study in teacher preparation programs, then these programs should also be modified according to the students' special needs.

In Israel, governmental bodies have made various attempts to adopt an inclusion policy. For example, in 2002, the Israel Knesset (the unicameral national legislature of Israel) approved the Integration Law (see Kolzchut, 2016) which states that students with special needs can participate in any academic/educational program offered by schools and higher-education institutions and must be provided with the required learning conditions/environments to achieve their goals.

From a practical point of view, existing programs must make various adjustments and accommodations in order to create the optimal conditions for effective inclusion. According to the Integration Law, each academic/ educational institution should create a special inclusion committee to profile the special needs of students and assist faculty in making the required modifications.

An analysis of the research literature on inclusion processes in teacher preparation indicates that most studies focus on two aspects—attitudes toward inclusion and programmatic changes/modifications. In one study (Swanson Gehrke & Cocchiarella, 2013), 125 pre-service elementary, secondary, and special education teachers were interviewed in order to identify aspects of university coursework and assigned field experiences that contributed to their ability to define, identify, and implement inclusion practices. The study documented a lack of consistency across teacher preparation programs in one university, and a disconnect between knowledge about inclusion as presented in university courses and inclusion practices observed in field experiences.

In another study (Forlin & Chambers, 2011), researchers examined pre-service teachers' perception of their preparedness for inclusion. They found that increasing knowledge about inclusion policies and improving levels of confidence in becoming inclusive teachers did not address teachers' concerns or their perceived stress about having students with disabilities in their classes. A third study (Oyler, 2011) described a teacher preparation program that prepared both single and dual certification master's students to teach in inclusive classrooms.

A few studies have examined the attitudes and perspectives of PE students toward inclusion (e.g., Hand, 2014); however, no studies have looked at the preparation of special needs students interested in becoming physical education teachers. Consequently, the Academic College at Wingate had to be creative in in approaching the inclusion challenge.

Dilemmas and Issues

In making adjustments for students with special needs, such as physical handicaps, vision impairments, or mental challenges, two main questions must be considered:

a. What actions should be taken to prepare the lecturers/instructors to work with these students?
b. What actions should be taken with the students at large so they can be part of a learning group composed of students with different needs?

A number of students with special needs have been accepted to the teacher preparation program at Wingate, among them students with various physical disabilities and a blind student. The aim was to enable these students to be part of a program composed of different types of studies—disciplinary studies (e.g., anatomy, motor learning, statistics), pedagogical studies (e.g., teaching methods/strategies, sports pedagogy, assessment of sport skills), physical activity classes (e.g., basketball, soccer, volleyball), and instructional/teaching practices in schools. In each type of class, modifications were needed.

Wingate's Response to the Challenge of Inclusion

After a number of applications were received from students with special needs, the board decided that the college should apply the Inclusion Law. This decision was made after examining the pros and cons of doing so. A special committee was appointed to advance this agenda.

Through a series of faculty meetings, senior faculty members brought the policy forward, explaining that the college was going to "open the gates" for students with special needs. In the beginning, it was difficult to discuss the inclusion issue since the college only offers a program in PE, a subject which requires students to attend lectures and participate in a variety of physical activity classes. Discussions focused on the importance of having students with special needs in the college as well as on how to handle the potential reactions of lecturers and other students.

As expected, there were a variety of reactions, including questions like these: Is it possible to plan a physical activity class composed of regular and handicapped students? How can a blind student play basketball? How can a physically handicapped student teach volleyball to a regular class of twelve-year-olds?

To address these questions, clinics were conducted by experts at the college who work in the area of adapted physical activity. In addition, examples of physical activities (e.g., ball games, basic gymnastics, folk dancing) for both "regular" students and students with special needs were demonstrated.

At the beginning of the semester, lecturers and instructors provided students with relevant information about the inclusion policy. They emphasized the benefits of the policy, but also discussed potential difficulties. Students were encouraged to share their feelings and perspectives. No personal information about students with special needs was provided.

A number of students were recruited to help the special needs students. Since most were studying adapted physical activity as a minor field, they were willing to assist in various capacities. This might involve studying with their special needs student at the library or at special learning zones at the college, working with them in the physical activity classes in order to help them learn the drills/skills, studying for exams together at home, giving them a ride home at the end of the day, and so on.

Modifications were also made in the lecture halls and activity classes so that special needs students had easy access to the rooms and could sit comfortably during lectures. Volunteer students sat next to special needs students and provided assistance if required. Lecturers were aware of students' special needs and met with them during the semester in special one-on-one sessions. In most cases, the volunteer students attended these sessions so that they would know what to work on.

The volunteer students met twice a term with members of the committee responsible for recruitment to report on their experiences, including challenges and difficulties, and how they approached them. For instance, when the volunteers accompanied the special needs students to their teaching assignments in schools, they did not know how much "freedom" to provide. Should they let the special needs student teach alone or intervene in the teaching process in order to help them get their message across to the pupils? They also raised questions about how to enable special needs students to be as independent as possible in their studies.

The volunteer students found that helping special needs students was a constructive experience, especially since they were minoring in adapted physical activity. In their PE teacher education classes, they learned about how to work with children with special needs. Spending time with special needs students helped them feel prepared to work with adults with special needs. They seemed to appreciate the opportunity.

Instructors who taught activity classes (e.g., basketball, soccer, track and field), were also aware of students' special needs. In cases where the student could not practice drills with the entire class, instructors prepared a special set of drills and allowed the special needs student to practice with their volunteer partner. Although time consuming, the preparation of extra drills was necessary to enable special needs students to practice the requisite motor skills. The modified drills were developed in cooperation with staff who were experts in adapted physical activity. Sports instructional aides (e.g., balls of different sizes) were used so that special needs students could practice motor tasks.

Once a semester, the students with special needs met with members of the recruitment committee and the volunteer students to describe their experiences in the program. The special needs students shared their thoughts and feelings about the program, including their experiences in and out of classes, described the challenges they faced as well as their personal and academic accomplishments, and offered their views about modifications in the program.

They also described the help they needed in order to improve their teaching skills. Like all students in the PE teacher preparation program, these students had "moments of success" and "moments of failure" in their field experiences. They were invited to elaborate on these experiences so that others could learn how to help them increase the number and frequency of "moments of success."

Members of the college staff responsible for the inclusion program met with key figures in the Ministry of Education, including the principal PE supervisor and the head of the unit for students with special needs to report on how the students with special needs were doing, consult on ways to improve the inclusion process, and discuss future teaching opportunities.

Some of the pedagogical concerns of lecturers and instructors were also discussed at these meeting. For example, all students in the program are required to teach instructional units in schools during the second and third years of the program. How should these field experiences be modified so that students with special needs could benefit most from their practical work in schools? Should they teach a small portion of the class? Should they teach with the assistance of a fellow student? Should they serve as assistants to the PE teacher at the school? Since there are no "right" answers to these questions, it was useful to hear perspectives and get advice from others.

To date, the special needs students at the Academic College at Wingate have not yet completed their four-year program. Some are classified as part-time students, which allows them to take fewer classes each year. Because these students may need some assistance when working in schools, hiring issues still need attention. Ideally principals who value the inclusion process and who are responsible for recruiting teachers to their schools should be invited to participate in such discussions.

ASSESSING THE EDUCATIONAL EFFORT: THE MISSING LINK

To date, no studies have been conducted on the multifaceted aspects associated with the inclusion of disabled students in PE teacher preparation programs. Any inclusion effort should be carefully evaluated to determine whether it is achieving its educational objectives. Presumably, such efforts have both educational merits and limitations (e.g., allocating a portion of the college's budget to address the challenge) that need to be analyzed and assessed.

Those involved in inclusion processes—policy makers, lecturers, and students—should be able to answer the following question: Was the effort worth it? In other words, did all the changes and modifications contribute to helping students with special needs achieve their goals?

To address this question, both quantitative and qualitative research is needed. The College plans to survey board members, faculty, and students as well as to collect stories about the experiences of students in the program. It will also be important to gather data from those who work with special needs students in the field—their supervisors, the regional PE supervisor, and principals. Such studies will help assess the program's strengths, determine how well it allows disabled students to gain disciplinary and pedagogical knowledge, and identify areas for improvement.

Integrating disabled students into a pre-service program for PE teachers presents unique challenges. Research is needed to increase understanding and inform program improvement. The Academic College at Wingate has taken on inclusion as part of its social and cultural mission. Future studies will provide useful evidence about the program and its impact.

REFERENCES

Clark, S. C. (2000). Work/family border theory: A new theory of work/family balance. *Human Relations, 53*, 747–770.
Council for Higher Education. (2016). *Statistical data.* Retrieved from http://www.che.org.il.
Forlin, C., & Chambers, D. (2011). Teacher preparation for inclusive education; increasing knowledge but raising concerns. *Asia-Pacific Journal of Teacher Education, 39*, 17–32.
Hand, K. E. (2014). Building confident teachers: Preservice physical education teachers' efficacy beliefs. *Journal of Case Studies in Education, 6*, 1–9.
Jobling, A., & Moni, K. B. (2004). I never imagined I'd have to teach these children: Providing authentic learning experiences for secondary preservice teachers in teaching students with special needs. *Asian-Pacific Journal of Teacher Education, 32*, 5–22.
Kolzchut (2016). *The Integration Law.* Retrieved from www.kolzchut.org.il/en/Children_with_Special_Needs.
Lidor, R., & Blumenstein, B. (2012). Soccer as a mediator for fostering relationships and building peace among Jewish and Arab players. In R. J. Schinke & S. J. Hanrahan (Eds.), *Sport for development, peace, and social justice* (pp. 39–55). Morgantown, WV: Fitness Information Technology.
Oyler, C. (2011). Teacher preparation for inclusive and critical (special) education. *Teacher Education and Special Education, 34*, 201–218.

Swanson Gehrke, R., & Cocchiarella, M. (2013). Preservice special and general educators' knowledge of inclusion. *Teacher Education and Special Education, 36,* 204–216.

Index

About the Editors and Contributors

EDITORS

Sharon Feiman-Nemser is the Jack, Joseph and Morton Mandel Professor of Jewish Education at Brandeis University, where she founded the Mandel Center for Studies in Jewish Education and the Master of Arts in Teaching (MAT) program. She also served on the education faculties at the University of Chicago and Michigan State University. A pioneer in research on teacher learning, she has written extensively on teacher education, learning to teach, mentoring, and new teacher induction. She is the author of *Teachers as Learners* (2012), a collection of her seminal writings. She was the first recipient of the Margaret Lindsey Award for Outstanding Research from the American Association of Colleges of Teacher Education (1996).

Miriam Ben-Peretz is Professor Emerita at the Faculty of Education at the University of Haifa, where she served as chair of the Department of Teacher Education and dean of the School of Education. She was also president of Tel-Hai College. Her main research interests are curriculum, teacher education and professional development, policy-making, and Jewish education. A member of the American National Academy of Education, Professor Ben-Peretz received AERA's Lifetime Achievement Award (Division C) and Legacy Award (Division K). She was the 2006 Laureate of the Israel Prize for Research in Education, and in 2015, she received the Israeli Prime-Minister's award, the EMET prize, for her contribution to educational research.

CONTRIBUTORS

Caroline Brennan is head of Secondary and Post Compulsory Teacher Education at the Cass School of Education and Communities, University of East

London, England. A former Secondary Modern Languages teacher in London, Caroline has had substantial experience leading and managing employment based routes to teaching.

Gerry Czerniawski is a reader in education at the Cass School of Education and Communities, University of East London, England. A former teacher, he runs the education doctoral programs at the University. Czerniawski currently chairs BERA's British Curriculum Forum, He is a National Teaching Fellow of the Higher Education Academy.

Francesca M. Forzani is associate director of TeachingWorks at the University of Michigan. She leads efforts to build curriculum materials and assessments for novice teachers focused on high-leverage teaching practices and has written about the history of teacher education and the practices-centered movement in teacher education.

Karen Symms Gallagher is the Emery Stoops and Joyce King Stoops Dean of the University of Southern California's Rossier School of Education. A leader in online learning models, Dean Gallagher has written numerous scholarly articles and four books. She received the Annual Award for "significant contributions to education innovation and reform in California" by 120 state school superintendents, the Dean's Superintendents Advisory Group.

Karen Hammerness is the director of Educational Research and Evaluation at the American Museum of Natural History. Her research focuses on the design and pedagogy of teacher education in the United States and internationally. She is especially interested in the pedagogies and preparation of teachers for specific settings, such as New York City and Chicago.

Ngaire Hoben is director of Secondary Teacher Education in the Faculty of Education and Social Work at the University of Auckland, New Zealand. A commitment to equity of outcome for school-aged learners informs and shapes her work with pre-service teachers.

Jae-Eun Joo earned her EdD from Harvard University. An associate professor in residence in the Neag School of Education at the University of Connecticut, she worked for Wide World, a global online professional development program for educators. She has extensive experience developing digital learning in various education contexts, including the use of digital technologies in the teaching of STEM subjects to Boston's urban youth.

Bill Kennedy is the assistant director of University of Chicago's Urban Teacher Education Program. He was a middle school teacher in New York City Public Schools and is a doctoral candidate at the University of Illinois at Chicago. His research focuses on the curriculum of teacher education and urban schools.

Warren Kidd is a senior lecturer at the Cass School of Education and Communities, University of East London, England, where he is a teacher educator in secondary and lifelong learning Initial Teacher Education programs. He also manages the Professional Standards Framework for the university, supporting academic staff across disciplines in their teaching.

Emily J. Klein is an associate professor at Montclair State University in the Department of Secondary and Special Education and member of the doctoral faculty. A former high school English teacher, she has written on teacher professional learning, teacher leadership, and urban teacher residencies. She is the co-author of *A Year in the Life of a Third Space Urban Teacher Residency: Using Inquiry to Reinvent Teacher Education* (2015).

Zipora Libman is the president of the Kibbutzim College of Education in Tel-Aviv, Israel. Her areas of expertise are assessment and research methodology in education. A former member of the Israeli Council of Higher Education, Libman has published numerous academic papers and books and worked to improve teacher training and policy issues in higher education.

Ronnie Lidor is a professor of motor behavior and the director of the Zinman College of Physical Education and Sport Sciences at the Wingate Institute in Israel. His main areas of research are motor learning, learning strategies, early development in sport, and sport development. Dr. Lidor has published over one hundred articles in peer-reviewed scientific journals, in addition to book chapters and proceedings in English and Hebrew.

Bob Moon is Emeritus Professor of Education at the Open University (UK). A former teacher and head teacher in two urban secondary schools, he has published extensively on curriculum and teacher education and served as advisor to national governments and international organizations including the EU, DFID, OECD, UNESCO, UNWRA, and the World Bank.

Jean Murray is a professor of education at the Cass School of Education and Communities, University of East London, England. Her research focuses on the sociological analysis of teacher education policies and practices with particular interests in teacher educators' identities and professional learning. She has written extensively, led numerous national and international research projects, and given many keynote lectures.

Margo Pensavalle, PhD, is professor of clinical education at the University of Southern California Rossier School of Education. A member of the design team for the MAT online Teacher Preparation Program, she is lead instructor in the course on Human Difference. Pensavalle taught in special needs and mainstream environments and served as a middle school principal. She holds a doctorate from the University of Southern California in Curriculum, Teaching, and Special Education.

Andrew Read is head of Primary Initial Teacher Education at the Cass School of Education and Communities, University of East London, England. He taught in primary schools in Tower Hamlets, London for fourteen years. He has written collaboratively on independent learning, with a particular focus on learner ownership of assessment. His chapter "Reflective Practice" is included in *Professional Studies in Primary Education* (2011).

Michal Shani is a lecturer at Levinsky College of Education in Israel. She is one of two academic leaders of Hotam Naomi Teacher Education Program. Her main research interests are teacher education, inclusive education, and instruction and learning processes for students with special needs.

Melora Sundt is a professor of clinical education at the University of Southern California's Rossier School of Education. She chaired the design teams for USC Rossier's blended MAT@USC, Global Executive EdD, and EdD in Organizational Change and Leadership programs. Besides teaching in USC Rossier's masters and doctoral programs, she blogs regularly about teaching online, organizational change, and preventing sexual assault.

Edith Tabak, PhD, was rector of Levinsky College of Education in Tel-Aviv, Israel. Previously she served as the head of the School of Education, in charge of curriculum development for pre- and in-service teachers. She was responsible for the College's partnership schools and relationship with Oranim College and the Hotam organization.

Eran Tamir is senior lecturer at Tel Aviv University School of Education and, formerly, an affiliated scholar at the Jack, Joseph and Morton Mandel Center for Studies in Jewish Education at Brandeis University. A sociologist and educational policy scholar, Tamir studies school leadership and culture, teacher careers and labor market, teacher preparation, and financial literacy. He co-edited *Inspiring Teaching: Preparing Teachers to Succeed in Mission-Driven Schools* (2014).

Monica Taylor is associate professor in the Department of Secondary and Special Education at Montclair State University and a member of the doctoral faculty. A former middle school Spanish/French teacher in New York City, her research focuses on urban education, teaching for social justice, and self-study. She is the co-author of *A Year in the Life of a Third Space Urban Teacher Residency: Using Inquiry to Reinvent Teacher Education* (2015).

Sara Shadmi-Wortman is one of the academic leaders of Hotam Naomi Teacher Education Program. She formerly served as head of the field department of Oranim College of Education in Israel, where she led the MA track for educational leadership in the community. Counselling for different countries regarding education as a tool for community change.